Pro-American Immigration

PRO-AMERICAN IMMIGRATION

Common Ground in our Immigration Strategy

GEORGE FARAG

LIONCREST
PUBLISHING

PRO-AMERICAN IMMIGRATION

Common Ground in our Immigration Strategy

ISBN   978-1-5445-0661-6 *Paperback*
       978-1-5445-0660-9 *Ebook*

Dedicated to

*My mom, Theresa, for keeping it together at
the airport so many years ago.*

My wife, Jenny, for encouraging me to make my voice heard.

and

*The American people, all of you, for allowing us to
arrive, survive, and thrive in the land of opportunity.*

CONTENTS

INTRODUCTION

Three generations of the same family are American citizens or green card holders—but none of them ever lived in the United States. How is that possible? This is neither a riddle nor a joke. This is an actual family, and they are not alone. There are thousands, if not tens of thousands, of similar families all over the world. The different generations of this kind of family illustrate the disrepair of our immigration system.

To be clear, I am not talking about illegal immigration—I am talking about our legal immigration system. Each year a million people use the legal immigration system to come to America. Most of the discussion on immigration today focuses on illegal immigration. But there are serious gaps in our legal immigration policies that are flying under the radar.

I would know—my family and I immigrated to America as one of the millions of families that came in pursuit of the American dream. We used the same immigration process that millions of others use all over the world.

I was also a United States diplomat and consular officer, or consul. It was my job to approve or deny immigrant and non-immigrant visa applications. I decided on thousands of visa applications while working at American embassies abroad. In each decision, I used US immigration law to guide me.

President George W. Bush appointed me to the diplomatic service. Secretary of State Condoleezza Rice confirmed me as a consul. I know the immigration process from the perspective of an immigrant and adjudicator.

Immigration is a hot topic. The situation is fluid, and it feels like immigration news is constantly breaking. As the 2020 presidential election approaches, news on immigration will probably move even faster. Writing about immigration in this atmosphere is challenging. As this book is being printed, there may be changes made to some of the policies explored in the text.

But the enduring principles in this book remain true—immigration to America must be controlled and consistent with US policy. Immigration policy must be to the benefit of America and the American people. The rules to process immigration applications must be consistent with immigration law. These are principles that all Americans can agree on. However, as we'll see in this book, these principles are not always the reality.

This is why my core message is that we need pro-American immigration. Pro-American immigration is immigration policy that puts the needs of Americans first. The idea is not to expand or limit immigration; it's to fix gaps in our current policies so that they are no longer exploited to the disadvantage of Americans. Pro-American immigration is good for all Americans—it is a common ground in the immigration debate.

WE THE PEOPLE

Immigration is politicized, and extreme points of view are framing the debate. Our lawmakers give the impression that every American is simply for or against immigration—all we hear is either build a wall or build a bridge, keep them out or let them in, and it's an invasion or there aren't enough.

It pains me to see such divisiveness in our country, and I don't think I am alone. I believe many Americans want an alternative. They want reasonable immigration policy that makes sense for all Americans. They want to offer solutions and not just complain about the issues.

The problem is that Congress can't get us there. In 2019, Senator Rick Scott (R-FL) described Congress by saying, "there's just so much hatred there right now and people aren't working together."[1] This hostile environment makes it impossible for lawmakers to have a productive debate on immigration.

This is why I am not recommending that we change our laws. To do so would require Congress to take action through a vote. In our current political environment, a snowball has a better chance of retiring in Miami than Congress has of agreeing on new immigration laws.

Instead, I recommend that American citizens, like you and me, lobby our government agencies for new regulations. Regulations are rules adopted by government agencies that determine how laws are enforced, and the United States encourages its citizens to lobby for these kinds of changes. This "citizen lobbying" is especially important when Congress is not working together.

For example, after the stock market crash of 1929, Congress passed the Securities and Exchange Act of 1934. This was a law that intended to control securities fraud and insider trading. But the Securities and Exchange Commission (SEC) still has its own regulations on how to enforce the law. So, while the law on securities fraud

---

1   Scott, "Meet the Press"

has remained constant, the regulations on responding to insider trading have changed.

The same is true about immigration. Immigration laws are already in place. The laws can remain the same—we should instead focus our attention on new regulations to enforce the law. That is where we can make a direct and immediate impact. We can do this by petitioning the appropriate government agencies for new regulations. They will determine how immigration laws are being enforced.

RECOMMENDATIONS FOR REASONABLE REGULATIONS

We want to have new immigration rules that make sense for all Americans. The American political system allows and encourages citizens to get involved. We can all affect change in immigration policy by making our voice heard through the petitioning process.

This process begins with getting our proposed rules on the agenda of regulation committees at each agency. A new rule or regulation must go before an authorized committee at the respective government agency. This is different than a new law, which needs a legislative sponsor in Congress. We will talk about how to get a new regulation implemented later in the book.

We will petition the US Department of State and US Citizenship and Immigration Services (USCIS) in Washington, DC. These are the two US government agencies most involved in the immigration process. The Department of State administers laws and implements policies related to visa services. USCIS administers the naturalization process to obtaining citizenship and also works on immigration.

Petitioning for new regulations requires effort—we must first understand the current policy, identify the gaps within it, and propose recommendations/regulations to fix those gaps. That is where this book comes in.

The world of immigration is complicated and intimidating. Reading text on immigration law is like reading a foreign language. Also, the majority of people talking about immigration are doing so in a partisan manner. In doing so, they are using the immigration debate to push an agenda. This makes understanding the facts of the immigration process difficult.

But I will simplify this for you. I will use my family's immigration story to illustrate how some people come to America. I will use my diplomatic experience with the US government to explain immigration policies. While I have my own political views, they will not be a part of this book.

This book will be a nonpartisan tool for you to understand how people come to America and how this process can be improved. We will discuss birthright citizenship, immigrant visas, fiancé visas, diversity visas, and green cards. In each of these areas you will learn the following:

1. How people legally come to America. We are bombarded with information about illegal immigration. But the majority of immigrants, over a million people, actually legally immigrate to America each year. I will use stories of how members of my own family came, and are still coming, to America. For those of you who do not know any families who recently immigrated, I invite you to get to know mine—we may be a little loud, but we are lovable. You can see some of the family members I am talking about in the family tree.

2. Gaps that exist in our current immigration policies. These gaps are to the disadvantage of the American people. We will need to discuss immigration laws and requirements in order to explore these gaps. However, I'm sure that you would prefer a root canal than to read about immigration law. To make this more manageable, I will use examples from my time as a consular officer. I will also use the "Consul's Corner" to summarize the laws we are discussing. You can refer to the "Consul's Corner" to find resources provided by the US Immigration and Nationality Act

(INA), US Citizenship and Immigration Services, and the US Department of State.

3. Proposals for new regulations to eliminate gaps in our immigration policy. The new rules presented will strengthen our legal immigration process in a way that benefits all Americans. They are a reasonable common ground in the immigration policy debate. The proposals culminate in a pro-American immigration plan.

I promise that, by the end of this book, you will have the confidence and knowledge to engage in the immigration debate. If you agree with pro-American immigration, I will ask you to be a part of our call for new regulations. If you disagree with some of the recommendations, I hope you will take action on the areas where you do agree. Together we can make our voices heard for a more pro-American immigration.

CHAPTER 1

———— ⭐ ————

A DEBT OF GRATITUDE

INTRODUCTION

There are many voices in the immigration debate—politicians are talking about immigration, journalists are talking about immigration, and immigrants are talking about immigration. It feels like everyone is talking about this issue. In such a crowded field, why should you listen to me?

My perspective on immigration reform is unique. I was an immigrant to America as well as a United States consul, or visa officer, with the State Department. I've been on both sides of the immigration process.

I immigrated to America with my family. I benefited from

the advantages of coming to the US and becoming an American citizen. For this, I owe the American people and US government a huge debt of gratitude.

I was also a US diplomat and consul with the US Department of State. I served at several US missions abroad. It was my job to approve or deny immigrant visa applications in line with US immigration law.

In this chapter, I will introduce you to parts of my personal journey as an immigrant. I will also discuss my professional experience as a diplomat. I want you to have a sense of what informs my perspective on immigration. This is important as we embark on our movement towards pro-American immigration.

COMING TO AMERICA

My family is from Alexandria, Egypt, and that is where I was born. We came to America, like millions of foreigners before us, to pursue the American dream for a better life. My father came to America as a graduate student. He was able to get lawful permanent residency (LPR) status upon finding a job after his studies. This meant he became a green card holder and could live and work in America. My mother, father, and I were all naturalized American citizens. In other words, we became US citizens through immigration—not birth. In contrast, my brother was born in America and is a US citizen through birth.

We settled in the neighborhood of South Boston, Massachusetts. "Southie" was a gritty, working-class, Irish-Catholic neighborhood. They used to joke that everyone in Southie was CIA: Catholic, Irish, and alcoholic. My family and I were not. We were DEA: Dreaming, Egyptian, and Arabs.

For those who know South Boston in the early 1980s, you will know that the area was violent. By the time I was nine years old, I witnessed two separate murders of African Americans below our house on D Street, which was across from the housing projects. In one case, a man was beaten to death outside the bar across the street. In the other case, a man was shot to death in his car just downstairs. I remember that the police knocked on our door to investigate the shooting. My mom was terrified to answer, but we could not ignore the cops.

I tried explaining to the police what I saw. I did not know the term "machine gun" yet, so I told him the guys used the same gun as the A-Team. *The A-Team* was one of my favorite television shows. I knew the fast gunshot sounds I heard in the street sounded like the weapon Mr. T used in the show.

As is the case for many immigrants, life was a challenge. My father complained about the stress of supporting a wife and two kids in the inner city. He felt like a stranger in a foreign land. There was constant bickering between my parents. My father abandoned us when I was seven years old. As he departed, I had a painful feeling that these were the last moments of us all being a family— and I was right.

My mother was left to fend for herself and two young boys in Boston's South End. She did her best to keep us happy, healthy, and protected. We had to come home after school and could never be outside after dark for any reason. There was always a cloud of anxiety that surrounded my family—my mom was afraid she could not protect us, and that same fear transmitted to my brother and me.

My father was not out of the picture completely. When he left us, he returned to Egypt. My mother saved quarters to be able to call him using a payphone down the street. She was looking for answers about how he could abandon us, as well as trying to reconcile with him. The sound of each quarter entering the payphone slot became a sound I associated with my father. I refused to speak to him on the phone or hear his voice. I refused to acknowledge that he left us alone in a place that we were seen as foreigners.

My mom took on different types of jobs. She worked as a cashier at a grocery store and she babysat neighborhood kids. But it was not enough—for all her good intentions, my mom could not take care of us on her own. She had to go on public assistance, or welfare. My mom is a very dignified woman, and I know that decision could not have been easy.

I did not know exactly what welfare was back then. I did not know how rent payments worked or why we could go to the doctor and not have to pay in cash like the other people. What I did know was that, at the store, some people paid in dollars but I paid with Monopoly-looking money. Back then, food stamps came in packets of one-, five-, ten-, and twenty-dollar bills in a variety of different colors.

It took me some time to understand that I could only buy food items with food stamps. A few times, store vendors made me put things back on the shelf such as crayons or toothpaste. I could not pay for them using food stamps, and it embarrassed me to put things back on the shelf. Even more than that, it scared me to not be able to buy things that we needed. I created a network of stores that allowed me to buy nonfood items with food stamps. In exchange, I had to pay a higher price for the items. Nonetheless, it was a big victory.

Our welfare ID also allowed us to have government cheese, butter, and powdered milk. My brother and I waited in line for hours in the schoolyard across the street from our apartment. When our turn came, we collected the blocks of cheese and butter. The government workers gave us enough for a three-member family.

One time, a fight broke out—I never knew what caused it. Groups of people were fighting, while others were trying to snatch food. My brother and I were close to the front of the line and I was able to grab a block of cheese. I had the cheese in one hand, and my brother's hand in the other, as we ran home. You may know the saying "bringing home the bacon," but for me it was "bringing home the cheese."

Those massive blocks of yellow American cheese lasted for weeks. The cheese did not come sliced, so we chopped off chunks it for dinner or other meals. Seeing those big, yellow blocks of cheese in our refrigerator gave me a sense of security that we had food. I don't know if it was a rational feeling or not, but I do know it felt good.

The government butter was also very meaningful for me. Every time my brother and I came home with the government butter, my mom used some of it to make us a homemade cake. I always licked the batter out of the bowl and loved the smell of the cake as it was being baked. The oven warmed the kitchen on cold Boston winter nights. My mom always had a big smile on her face because she knew her homemade cake was our favorite. The experience gave me a wonderful sense of well-being.

I looked forward to the "government" coming to provide us cheese, butter, and milk. At a young age, I began to understand the role of the American government in our lives. I realized that it was assisting in our survival. Even today, when I am at a deli and I see the blocks of yellow cheese, a smile comes to my face. Now I can afford to buy sliced deli cheese, but the kid that was grateful to the government for giving us cheese in a public school courtyard still lives in me.

ESCAPING EGYPT

We had to pack the car at night while the neighbors were sleeping. We could not take the risk that the news of our departure would reach my father. It was October 1986, and my mother, brother, and I were escaping from Egypt. We had spent the previous year in Egypt as my mother tried to reconcile their marriage. My mother is an old-school Egyptian woman and could handle the prospect of not having a husband. But the idea of her children not having a father felt like too much to handle. She wanted to try and convince my father to return to the family and help raise his children.

I loved it in Alexandria. I enjoyed being close to family and felt safe there. Street crime was very rare, so the prospect of witnessing another murder was nonexistent. But after fifteen months, it was evident that my father was not interested in maintaining a family. By the end of our time in Egypt, my family was scattered. I was living with my grandmother, while my mom and brother were living with my mother's sister. My father did not want us in the house.

My mom's efforts to reunite our family had failed. She knew that the children of a poor, single mother in Egypt had almost no opportunity for a better life. We had to get out of Egypt and back to the US.

But there was a problem—Egyptian law allowed a father to prevent his wife and children under eighteen from leaving the country. My father was not interested in taking on the responsibilities of being a father or having a family. He did not want to pay for our schooling, take part in disciplining us, or even have us living in his house. Still, he did want to flex his macho muscles in other ways.

We feared that, in a demonstration of virility, he would not allow us to leave the country. We could not tell him we were planning to leave Egypt—we feared he would place a travel restriction request with the Egyptian authorities.

Therefore, we had to leave without him knowing. Alexandria was a small place where rumors spread fast, and we could not risk rumors of our departure reaching my father. So we had to leave Alexandria in the middle of the night. My uncle and his cousin packed the car in the darkness. While the neighborhood of Moharam Beyk slept, everyone inside my grandmother's house was awake. My mother, aunts, and grandmother wept as they said their goodbyes.

I tried my best to put on a strong face. There was a feeling of cold emptiness inside me. I did not want to leave. As I said my goodbye to my grandmother, she told me I was now the man of the house. At eleven years old, I felt that my mom and younger brother were now my responsibility. I did my best to hold back the tears, but, when she hugged me, it was like a floodgate exploded inside my eyes.

In spite of this sadness, I knew that, if we were not able to get back to America, our future was in serious jeopardy. Everyone was whispering with the lights dimmed to be careful not to wake up the neighbors in the building. We were almost out of the door when my aunt Margo called my name. She ran to the kitchen and brought back a jar of my favorite homemade date jam that she had made for me. I put it in my bag, and our journey back to America began.

We departed Alexandria for Cairo International Airport in the still darkness. The only other beings that were awake were the cats finding their next meal in the garbage. The desert road connecting Alexandria to Cairo had no streetlights. I couldn't see anything, except for occasional taillights of another car. I pretended that they were fireflies in the distance that we were chasing.

It was a quiet journey—my uncle drove in silence and my mom spent most of the time looking out of the window at the passing sand. There was an occasional brief conversation between my uncle and his cousin in the passenger's seat. My younger brother was asleep on my mother's lap. After a four-hour journey, we arrived in Cairo at around the same time as the sun was beginning to rise. I remember seeing the tips of the Great Pyramids of Giza in the distance. I knew of them, but in the year we spent in Egypt, we never visited.

Once we reached Cairo, the conversation in the car increased. My uncle joked around, saying that he wished he could come with us to America in one of our suitcases. He was trying to keep my mom's mind off of the forthcoming encounter with the Egyptian authorities at the airport.

As we got closer to the airport, the topic was finally breached. The customs and border control officer at the airport could do several things—he could ask for a travel authorization from my father or could find that we were on the travel restriction list. He could even request that our father come to the airport, even if he was not traveling. My mother had to be very careful. The possibility that she might be arrested for child abduction became very real.

My uncle kept telling my mom to remain calm and insist on speaking with "the consul" if anything happened. It was my first time to hear the word consul. I did not know what a consul was. It sounded like someone who had authority. I had no clue that I would one day become one of them.

It felt like an eternity as we stood in line and watched the customs officer point to person after person to come forward. The closer we got to the front, the sweatier my mom's hands became. Finally, our turn came and we made the longest ten-foot walk of our lives to the officer's booth. My mother then gave the border security officer our US passports and boarding passes.

He looked at her and asked if she spoke Arabic. She said yes. He continued to stare and asked where our Egyptian passports were. My mom explained calmly that we did not have Egyptian passports—she did not renew them since we had American ones. He asked what the purpose of our trip was, and my mom said, "We are going home." The officer then asked, "Where is your husband?" My mom must have practiced this moment a thousand times in her mind. She must have thought of several answers and weighed the repercussions of each one.

She looked him straight in the eye and said, "He is waiting for us." I would later understand the genius of her response. The officer could assume that my father was waiting for us in America. But my mother never specified where exactly my father was. In doing so, she could not be accused of lying to a government official. It was up to the officer to make an assumption or ask further questions.

The officer nodded his head, scooped up our passports, and told us to wait there. He walked to an office at the far of the vast immigration hall. The intensity of the situation made my heart race. I looked up towards my mom who was still holding my brother. She looked down to me. It was the first time she looked at me since we arrived at the booth. She smiled and said, "It is fine. This is normal."

However, in fact, this was not normal. He did not leave his booth for any of the people whom he processed before us. After minutes that felt like hours, the officer returned and sat down. In one quick action, he stamped all our passports. The sound of the metal stamp slamming against the passport pages rang in my ear.

Our boarding gate had not yet been announced, since we arrived at the airport so early. We found a quiet space in the airport and sat. The hard plastic chairs were uncomfortable and did not allow us to lie down. Instead, my mom laid her red coat on the floor so that I could sleep on it. The exhaustion of the overnight drive and stress of not knowing what would happen to my mom took a toll on me. I fell asleep on the airport floor for what felt like only a few minutes, but in reality it was hours.

We boarded the Egypt Air flight to John F. Kennedy International Airport in New York. As the plane finally took off from Cairo, my mom began to cry. It was a combination of sadness of leaving her family, fear of what was to come, and relief that we made it out. All I could do was put my arm around her and say, "Thank you."

Our US citizenship tipped the scale in our favor at the airport. The US government had once again come to our rescue. It was time for a new beginning.

GENEROSITY OF THE AMERICAN PEOPLE

When we arrived in America we moved to Jersey City, New Jersey. Jersey City (JC) was also a rough neighborhood when we moved there. It was common to find heroin needles in the street. Cars were placed on cinder blocks at night while the rims were stolen. A man named Buddha and his two pit bulls were the law around our block.

My mother found a small, rent-controlled apartment. The apartment had enough space to fit three small beds. My mother, brother, and I slept in the same room until I went to college. Most of our furniture was secondhand. For example, we found a small round office table in the garbage that we used as a kitchen table. We created many great memories around that table.

The people of JC were a diverse group of blue-collar, working-class families. Many were immigrants who recently arrived in the US. Anyone could fit in JC—and that was my favorite thing about it. It is where I became an adult and continues to be my hometown.

The United States government continued to be present in our lives in Jersey City. I went to Public School Number 24 (P.S. 24), which is now called Chaplain Charles Watters Elementary School. I began working at the local grocery store on the corner when I was twelve years old. I studied hard and was valedictorian of my eighth-grade class.

During eighth grade, I could not sleep on many nights. I dreaded the idea of going to high school. Our district high school was infamous for violence. It was commonplace to hear of people being attacked, or even killed, in and around the school. This high school installed metal detectors for guns long before it was commonplace to do so.

I was not a tough guy, but we did not have the money for me to attend private school. I worried about how I would navigate the next four years in a school where drugs and violence were the norm. Once again the US government came to the rescue—I was accepted to a government-funded magnet school called Academic High School. My acceptance letter to Academic High was my ticket to being able to calmly sleep at night.

Attending the magnet school meant that I could study in an insulated environment, away from the daily dangers of the inner city. It was also the first tangible example in my life that proved that, if I put in the effort, America would reward me. Today, Academic High School is known as Dr. Ronald E. McNair Academic High School. It is one of the best high schools in New Jersey. As far as I am concerned, it is the best high school in the world.

While in high school, I benefited from other public-private partnership programs. In these partnerships, private organizations cooperated with government agencies to offer educational and professional programming. I attended the Saint Peter's College summer Pre-College Academic Program (Pre-Cap). Pre-Cap allowed us to practice mathematics and science skills during the summer. This allowed Jersey City youth, like me, to stay off the streets and stay out of trouble.

The program also provided me with many firsts. It was the first time I attended a professional baseball game and rooted for the New York Yankees. It was the first time I went water rafting. It was the first time I acted on stage and saw the splendor of a Broadway play *(Miss Saigon)*. The Pre-Cap program, and the government funding, allowed me to experience all these things at that moment of my life.

The US government also played a critical role in my university experience. I received the New Jersey state-funded Garden State Scholarship. With the scholarship, I attended The College of New Jersey (TCNJ). TCNJ offered me a solid undergraduate education and the opportunity to study abroad. As a result, I studied in Seville, Spain, and Quito, Ecuador.

Going to Seville was a turning point in my life. Seville is a beautiful city, and I was fortunate enough to be there during the spring semester. I could smell the orange blossoms on the cobblestone streets of el Barrio de Santa Cruz. I walked to the university every day and admired the Moorish architecture. I had lunch, which my host family packed for me, at the Plaza d'España, where tourists gazed at the detailed mosaics. I took flamenco dance classes with Carmen y Carmen and loved every second of it. Many times I pinched myself to believe I was actually there. I could not believe that I went from an American inner city to the streets of Seville.

The American people and government were very kind to my family and me. My father had abandoned us, but American taxpayer dollars helped to keep a roof over our heads and food in the refrigerator. Public schools and scholarships provided an education for my brother and me. My mother's grit, and the US government's assistance, allowed me to go from standing in line for government cheese to dancing flamenco in Spain. I felt grateful and indebted to both my mom and our government.

DEMONSTRATING MY GRATITUDE

On a beautiful morning in September 2001, I was at home preparing for my drive back to Syracuse University. While doing so, I turned on the television and saw the images of the Twin Towers in New York City with smoke billowing out of them. Like many people, I thought this was the trailer of a movie. I soon realized it was real—and I could not believe what I was seeing. Suddenly, the South Tower of the World Trade Center began to collapse. I felt like I wanted to throw up.

I ran up to the roof of our apartment building in Jersey

City. There, I could see the smoke coming out of lower Manhattan. By the time the North Tower collapsed, it was obvious that the world had changed. My world changed. As I looked on in horror and grief, I felt very small. We were under attack—and all I could do was watch. In the midst of the chaos, I had a moment of peace. I realized that, after all the time that the United States had spent in serving me, it was now time for me to serve the United States.

I became determined to become a diplomat for America. I wanted to represent the United States and our interests abroad. I took the Foreign Service written exam after the September 11 attacks. The exam was administered at a local high school on a Saturday. A blue exam book and a bubble sheet were distributed to everyone in the classroom. I took out two pencils and a pencil sharpener. I sat in a high school classroom and began filling in the bubbles. I felt like I was taking the SAT on steroids—I grappled with questions on geography, English, history, math, economics, culture, and more. When I finished the exam, I felt completely drained.

I passed the written exam on the first attempt. After that, I had other oral exams and interviews that I also passed. Then, a full security clearance investigation was done on my background. Special agents from the US National Background Investigations Bureau talked to people that knew me in every place I had lived—from Jersey City to Cairo to Seville. They talked to my former professors, colleagues, and friends. They checked my credit, tax background, and criminal history. The US government knew more about me than my own family did.

I received my top-secret security clearance. The clearance gave me access to classified information. This included information about national security, counterterrorism, and other sensitive data. I was cleared for worldwide service except Egypt. I could not serve in a diplomatic position in Egypt for at least five years due to my Egyptian background.

I was ecstatic to become a US diplomat and consular officer with the US Department of State. I could serve the US government and American people who had given me so much.

SERVING AMERICA

Going from the streets of Jersey City to the halls of US embassies took some adjusting. My first posting was at the US embassy in the Kingdom of Bahrain in the Persian Gulf.

The US ambassador to Bahrain, Ronald E. Neumann, came from a storied diplomatic family. He was the son of a former ambassador and traveled around the world with his family. Both he and his father served in diplomatic posts in Afghanistan. The only other father/son pair to serve at a diplomatic mission was John Adams and his son John Quincy Adams—they both served as ministers to Britain.

Ambassador Neumann was a good man, but we did not have much in common. The ambassador came from a diplomatic family. I came from a single-mother, welfare family. The ambassador's family traveled to represent America abroad. My family fought to enter America. The ambassador had something in common with John Quincy Adams (the sixth president of the United States), and I had only been to Quincy Market in South Boston. We did have one thing in common, though—a desire to serve our country.

I served in Bahrain at a sensitive time. The US Navy Fifth Fleet, based in Bahrain, evacuated 1,000 people in three days. At the same time, the US embassy also authorized the departure of personnel, a response to threats related to six suspected terrorists with ties to Al Qaeda.

The terrorists were suspected to be linked to the bombings of three residential compounds in Saudi Arabia, just across the bridge from Bahrain. The bombings killed thirty-nine people and injured 160. The movie *The*

Kingdom, starring Jamie Foxx, eventually used these bombings as a backdrop for the story. The terrorists were suspected of planning bombings in Bahrain. In spite of the evacuation, I remained at the embassy to carry out essential services.

In 2003, I volunteered to transfer to the Department of Defense. I served as part of the Coalition Provisional Authority (CPA) in Iraq. This was at the height of Operation Iraqi Freedom. CPA was the transitional government after the fall of Saddam Hussein's Ba'ath regime. CPA had executive, legislative, and judicial authority over the Iraqi government. This jurisdiction lasted from CPA's inception on April 21, 2003, until its dissolution on June 28, 2004.

I had no military training—only two hours of weapons instruction with the regional security officer (RSO) at the US embassy in Bahrain. Nonetheless, I boarded a C-130 military transport plane into Baghdad. I was one of the first US diplomats in post-Saddam Hussein Iraq.

I lost eleven brothers and sisters at arms in different ambushes in Iraq. Those murders hit me hard, but I kept fighting for my country and myself. I negotiated the release of an ambassador that was being held by a mob. I avoided being kidnapped myself by the local insurgent militia in Najaf, Iraq.

After Iraq, I served in Beirut, Lebanon, as a US consul. I made decisions on thousands of immigrant and non-immigrant visa applications. I was there during the 2006 Lebanon War and on the Consular Affairs Crisis Response team that evacuated 15,000 Americans from Beirut. It was one of the largest overseas evacuations of Americans in recent history.

The evacuation was so large and sudden that it required the help of the Department of Defense (DoD). We needed the DoD's expertise to locate and transport Americans out of sensitive areas. We also needed the DoD's sea and air vessels. We had six helicopters, the USS Nashville, the USS Iwo Jima, and private cruise ships transporting Americans out of Lebanon.

I chose to serve as a US diplomat in challenging countries under difficult conditions. There were times when things were particularly tough. In these moments, I thought back to the help the American people and government gave my family and me to survive. My service in these areas of conflict was the least I could do to show my gratitude.

CONCLUSION

My passion to repay my debt of gratitude to the United States also informed my decision to write this book. The debate on immigration is tearing our country in two different directions—but there is space for a common ground.

I lived in the United States as an immigrant and with immigrants. I know exactly how immigrating to America, and becoming a US citizen, can impact one's life. Immigrating to the US changed my life—it may have actually saved my life. The pursuit of the American dream is something I wish for everyone who desires it.

At the same time, I have also been a US consul—one who served at embassies abroad and made decisions on immigrant visas. I learned about US immigration law. I saw shortcomings in immigration policy that are not to the advantage of Americans.

In the next chapter, we will dive deeper into my experience as a US consul. We will explore lessons I learned about the immigration process. It is these lessons that inform my desire for pro-American immigration.

CHAPTER 2

★

LESSONS LEARNED AS A CONSUL

INTRODUCTION

The day I took the oath of office to become a United States diplomat was one of the proudest days of my life. I took the same oath that our first secretary of state, Thomas Jefferson, took over two centuries ago. As a US consul, our government entrusted me with the power to approve or deny people to come to America. It was a responsibility that I took very seriously.

I interviewed thousands of people who applied for visas to America. Some were nervous, while others were relaxed. Some wanted to visit friends in Chicago, and others wanted to live in California. Some were honest, and some were not so honest.

In each visa interview, I learned something. I gained a deeper understanding of the nature of human beings, honed my decision-making skills, and saw the importance of strong policy. I had a behind-the-scenes look into the situations abroad that influence our lives at home.

In this chapter, I will present some of the lessons I learned about immigration while I was a US consul. These lessons led me to identify holes in immigration laws that don't benefit Americans and informed my approach to pro-American immigration.

LESSON ONE: THERE ARE GAPS IN OUR IMMIGRATION POLICIES

I trained to become a US consul at the Foreign Service Institute (FSI) in Arlington, Virginia. We studied immigration law and nonimmigrant visa regulations. The foundation of our studies was the Immigration and Nationality Act (INA).

The INA was enacted in 1952 and provides the legal structure for immigration. It has been amended many times over the years. It contains many of the most important provisions of immigration law. The INA is in the US Code, which is a collection of all the laws of the United States.

We learned questioning techniques to conduct efficient

interviews. We became experts at making swift decisions. Security of the homeland was our main focus, but we also had to maintain an openness to people who wanted to legally come to America.

While working at embassies abroad, I made decisions on thousands of visa applications. As I put my training into practice, I found that there are gaps in our visa policy. For example, parents use tourist visas to give birth in America. Additionally, afterward, they are still able to qualify for further tourist visas in the future. Sponsors of family-based immigrants are only required to have income that is less than the threshold to receive food stamps. Even green card holders who are not living in the US can still sponsor other immigrants to come to America.

These gaps are not helpful to Americans nor aligned with the intention of the immigration law. This is problematic.

LESSON TWO: FOREIGN VISA APPLICANTS ARE SAVVY

Foreign visa applicants are very knowledgeable of US immigration law. I found that most foreigners know more about our immigration law than the average American. They know about the loopholes in our policies and use them to their advantage. Foreigners know that if they give birth in the US on a tourist visa, their child will become an American—which will benefit both the child and the parent.

Foreigners who have green cards know that they don't have to live in America to maintain their legal permanent resident status. They know that if they have a green card, they can help other family members immigrate to America. It does not matter if they are living in another country—and, if they have a green card for five years, they can qualify for even more benefits.

They know that these loopholes are not what the law intends and don't function in the interest of the American people. But they also know that they are not acting illegally—they are following the letter, but not the spirit, of the law.

Some people may fault foreigners for doing this. However, in other contexts, people who are able to play the system to their benefit are often considered smart. A good example of this comes from the National Football League (NFL) in the United States.

In 2016, a player for the Green Bay Packers, Ty Montgomery, exploited an NFL rule to his team's advantage. On a kickoff, the ball was kicked towards the end zone. It appeared that the Packers would start on their own five-yard line. Instead, the ball went into the playing field. Montgomery purposefully went out of bounds and fell on the ball. As a result of this move, the Packers instead started from their own forty-yard line and ended up scoring.

Montgomery manipulated the rules to his advantage. The intention behind the NFL's creation of this rule was different from how Montgomery used it. It was a "smart" loophole—and the Packers have continued to use this rule to their advantage on multiple occasions.

The rule has been called bizarre and idiotic. Yet the players who manipulate the rules are not looked down upon. Instead, Montgomery was called "brilliant." Despite misuse, the rule still exists, and teams can still take advantage of it. You can't hate Ty Montgomery for taking advantage of the rule—but you can fault the NFL leadership for not closing the gap in the regulations.

I have also taken advantage of loopholes myself. When I was a freshman in college, I applied for an internship program. The program was only available to Latino and African American students. Even though I knew this, I still applied, but as an African American.

My interviewer was surprised because, although my application stated that I was African American, I was not black. I explained that I was African American because I was born in Egypt. Egypt is on the continent of Africa. I was Egyptian American and thus African American. He laughed and said, "I guess you have a point."

I was accepted to the program—I had played the system and was rewarded. I received an amazing internship at an investment firm that lasted throughout my college years. I made wonderful friends in the program and my peers affectionately referred me to as "Mr. African American."

Montgomery exploited rules to get a better field position. I exploited the rules to earn an internship. In the same vein, immigrants also know and exploit the immigration laws for their own advantage.

LESSON THREE: AMERICANS ARE CONCERNED

When I was with the State Department, I liked being a hometown diplomat. That meant I visited schools, government officials, and local media in America. I talked with the audience about issues related to my work as a diplomat. For many people, I was the first US diplomat they had ever met. It was an opportunity for others to learn about the world of diplomacy and for me to hear their thoughts. We talked about everything—however, the majority of people I talked to had concerns about immigration.

LOWER WAGES

"Immigrants take American jobs and lower our wages." I heard this statement from Judy. Judy is in her mid-thirties, is a mother of two wonderful kids, and lives in Pennsylvania. She volunteers at the local Salvation Army and does her best to raise her kids to respect others. Judy knows that immigration is a sensitive issue. She had classmates, colleagues, and neighbors who immigrated to America. She understands and respects their desire for the American dream.

At the same time, Judy also worries that "chain immigration" will further drain local resources. She decided to go back to work after her second child went to kindergarten, but she had difficulty finding a job. The fact that she was unable to find a suitable job bothered her—but it is the idea that her children may struggle to thrive in the future that really keeps her up at night.

"As more people come in, our limited resources are stretched even further. Things are already hard, and they will get harder for my kids," she told me. Judy represents many with the same concern. She does not harbor negativity towards individual immigrants, yet the idea of uncontrolled immigration scares her. She feels it threatens the prosperity of her family.

A common concern is that immigrants are a drain on tax dollars. Some people believe that immigrants are using millions of dollars in public assistance, or welfare, programs. Helen administers public assistance programs in St. Louis, Missouri. She explained that immigrants can use some public assistance programs. For example, the Supreme Court ruling *Plyer v. Doe* allows all immigrant children to attend public schools for grades K-12. It does not matter if they are in the US legally or illegally.

Immigrant parents can also use federal assistance for children who meet eligibility requirements. For example, Magy uses food stamps to feed her children healthy meals. Magy is in the country illegally, but her children are US citizens. She receives $300 a month from the Supplemental Nutrition Assistance Program (SNAP) for her two children.

Illegal immigrants may also use public resources. For example, they can use emergency Medicaid and treatment in hospital emergency rooms. They have access to healthcare and nutrition programs like the Women, Infants, and Children (WIC) nutrition program.

For Helen, she understands the motivation of immigrants to request federal assistance programs. She sees firsthand that, for many, it is a matter of survival for themselves and their children. Still, it bothers her that the tax dollars of Americans are going to support families of legal and illegal immigrants. "My family and I are already living month to month. It doesn't feel fair for us to support people whose own governments are doing nothing for them," she confided.

IMPACT ON CRIME

There is a perception that immigrants are a major source of crime in the United States. In 2018, the University of Chicago and Washington University conducted a study. Researchers Flores and Schachter surveyed 1,500 non-Hispanic whites throughout the United States.

The respondents received profiles of different immigrants with randomly assigned traits. The traits included national origin, age, gender, occupation, and criminal history. They asked the participants if they thought these immigrants were in the US legally or illegally. The respondents classified Latin Americans, Africans, and Middle Easterners as "illegal." It didn't matter what their actual documentation status was.[2]

There are examples of bad individuals who contribute to this perception and, therefore, fuel the media attention on immigrants. For example, in October 2017, Sayfullo

---

2   Flores and Schachter, "Who are the Illegals."

Saipov killed eight people in New York City. He drove a truck into a bike path close to the World Trade Center. Saipov legally immigrated to the United States from Uzbekistan in 2010. In August 2018, Cristhian Rivera allegedly murdered a twenty-year-old Iowa college student. Rivera entered the United States from Mexico as an undocumented immigrant.

As a person with a Middle Eastern background, it pains me to know that some Americans categorize me in the same group as these terrorists. On the other hand, I do understand how these high-profile incidents ignite a fear of immigrants.

NATIONAL IDENTITY

Others worry that America could lose its identity by shutting its door to immigrants. For example, John is a teacher in Chicago. He fears that the United States is changing from being known as a "nation of immigrants."

John appreciates that immigrants have made major contributions to America. Immigrants have contributed to our economy, infrastructure, and culture. "Immigrants built America's railroads, skyscrapers, and farming industries. Immigrants are a major reason our software industry is world-class," he told me. John is frustrated that they are not more celebrated.

The US government is taking steps to move away from the country's association with the image John describes. USCIS is the federal agency tasked with managing immigration to America. In February 2018, it changed its mission statement by eliminating a passage that describes the United States as "a nation of immigrants." The old mission statement of USCIS reads as follows:

> USCIS secures America's promise as a **nation of immigrants** by providing accurate and useful information to our customers, granting immigration and citizenship benefits, promoting an awareness and understanding of citizenship, and ensuring the integrity of our immigration system. (emphasis added)

The new mission statement reads as follows:

> US Citizenship and Immigration Services administers the nation's lawful immigration system, safeguarding its integrity and promise by efficiently and fairly adjudicating requests for immigration benefits while protecting Americans, securing the homeland, and honoring our values.

Some Americans feel that it is America's duty to uphold the ideal expressed in Emma Lazarus's sonnet "The New Colossus," the words of which are immortalized on the Statue of Liberty. It reads, "Give me your tired, your poor, your huddled masses yearning to breathe free." Many believe we have a moral responsibility to help refugees as many are fleeing persecution at the hands of their own governments.

One such American is Justine from Austin, Texas. Justine is a caseworker for refugees in her state. She believes that we cannot turn our back on refugees who want to come to America in search of a better life. She sees the desperation of refugees every day and wants to find a solution to bring as many of them as possible into America. She thinks that part of America's identity is being a place that can provide individuals with a better future.

HURTING OUR PROMINENCE IN THE WORLD

Other Americans fear that discouraging immigration will hurt our prominence in the world. America is the place that intellectuals and entrepreneurs come to pursue their ambitions. One of these intellectuals was the Nobel Prize recipient Dr. Ahmed Zewail.

Zewail was born and raised in Egypt. He moved to the US and joined the California Institute of Technology (Caltech). In 1982, Zewail became a naturalized citizen of the United States. In 1999, he won the Nobel Prize in Chemistry.

I attended a speech Zewail gave about his Nobel Prize win

at the American University of Cairo in 1999. He credited his immigration to the United States as the thing that gave him the opportunity to even be in a position in which he could earn the award. He called America the "gateway to bigger dreams."

He spoke passionately about his decision to immigrate, saying, "America was second to none in the opportunities it offered, especially to young people. Besides the rich and free culture, there was the feeling that the sky was the limit." Certain Americans fear our country will miss out on people like Dr. Zewail if we limit immigration.

ECONOMIC IMPACT

There is also the fear that restricting immigration will negatively impact our economy. For example, the technology ecosystem is a vital part of the US economy. The important role of immigrants in American technological innovation is well-documented. Immigrants have founded many of the major technology companies in the United States, such as Google, Yahoo, Tesla, eBay, Qualcomm, VMware, and PayPal.

Immigrant-founded companies in the US employ more than 12.8 million people worldwide. They account for more than $5.3 trillion in global revenue. In 2016, over half of the eighty-seven tech "unicorns," private companies valued at more than $1 billion, were co-founded by immigrants. Each of these companies had created an average of 760 jobs.[3] Limiting immigration could limit growth in the technology sector.

LESSON FOUR: BEWARE OF COMPREHENSIVE REFORM

Republican and Democratic politicians understand that there is a need for immigration reform. But they subscribe to a common idea among diplomats: "Nothing is agreed until everything is agreed." They want comprehensive immigration reform. Comprehensive immigration reform is one piece of legislation that tackles all three pillars of immigration policy:

1. Strengthening the rule of law

2. Supporting border security and law enforcement

3. Dealing with illegal immigrants that are already in the United States

In May 2006, President George W. Bush said, "I support comprehensive immigration reform..."[4] However there was no comprehensive immigration reform in 2006.

---

3   Anderson, "Immigrants and Billion Dollar Startups."

4   White House, "President Bush Addresses the Nation on Immigration Reform."

In January 2013, President Barack Obama said, "We still need to pass comprehensive immigration reform that addresses our twenty-first century economic and security needs."[5] Still, there was no comprehensive immigration reform in 2013.

In January 2018, President Donald Trump said, "Comprehensive immigration reform...is where I would like to get to eventually."[6] Yet again, there was no comprehensive immigration reform in 2018.

The last time there was comprehensive immigration reform was in 1986. President Ronald Reagan signed into law the Immigration Reform and Control Act (IRCA) in November 1986. The act was also known as the Reagan Amnesty. This was the last time that one piece of immigration legislation was "comprehensive" or, in other words, addressed all of the pillars.

IRCA established federal civil and criminal penalties for employers who hired illegal immigrants. Employers had to verify the authorization to work of all new hires, including US citizens. This was part of pillar one—strengthen the rule of law.

IRCA established new criminal penalties for fraudulent

5   Obama, "Remarks by the President on Immigration."

6   Wilkie, "Trump Says He'll Sign DACA Deal, Pursue Comprehensive Immigration Reform."

use of identity documents. It also created penalties for transporting or harboring unauthorized immigrants. It increased funding for the Immigration and Naturalization Service (INS). This was used to handle immigration enforcement by increasing the number of border patrol agents by 50 percent. These actions were part of pillar two—to support border security and law enforcement.

IRCA instituted an amnesty program that allowed some illegal immigrants to apply for legal status. They had to have been present in the United States since January 1, 1982, and meet certain conditions. These applicants could even qualify for US citizenship. President Reagan saw this as a solution for the illegal immigrant problem. It would enable unauthorized immigrants to come out of the shadows and "step into the sunlight."[7] This was part of pillar three—to deal with illegal immigrants that are already in the United States.

IRCA was the last time comprehensive immigration reform passed. Since then, there has been only one attempt to pass comprehensive immigration reform. In 2013, Senator Chuck Schumer (D-NY) and the "Gang of Eight" drafted the Border Security, Economic Opportunity, and Immigration Modernization Act. The "Gang of Eight" was a bipartisan group of US senators—four were Democrats and four were Republicans.

---

7   Reagan, "Statement on Signing the Immigration Reform and Control Act of 1986."

The draft law stated that the bill provided for "comprehensive immigration reform and for other purposes." It addressed all of the three pillars.

In regards to pillar one, it required all employers to confirm employee work authorization and would provide an improved employment verification system to do so.

Concerning pillar two, the legislation planned for investments in border security. It would deploy at least 38,000 full-time border patrol agents along the southern border and create an electronic exit system at all US ports. Additionally, it called for constructing at least 700 miles of fencing along the southern border.

Finally, for pillar three, the bill allowed a path to citizenship for illegal immigrants. To be considered for this, they had to already be in the United States and would also have to wait for current legal immigrants to receive their green cards first.

The United States House of Representatives did not act on the bill and it died at the end of the 113th Congress in 2013. This attempt at comprehensive immigration reform failed due to a lack of agreement among our legislators.

Our political leaders have repeated comprehensive immigration reform as a vision—it is a great sound bite. In reality, this vision has not led to any meaningful change in our immigration policy for over thirty years.

In this polarized climate, it would be difficult for everyone to agree on everything. It is improbable to comprehensively reform immigration in one idea, policy, or law. If we wait on everything to be agreed upon, nothing will be. This is not sustainable—instead, we should focus on reasonable ideas on immigration policy reforms. This will create a common ground to help move the issue forward.

FAST FIXES FIRST

I previously spoke of how there are gaps in our legal immigration rules. Foreigners are using these gaps to their advantage, and this makes Americans concerned. There is a need for reform in our immigration processes. In the meantime, politicians love using the concept of comprehensive immigration reform—it sounds good and is the ideal solution. But nothing has happened in over thirty years and will likely not happen anytime soon. We need action on immigration reform now—we can do so by focusing first on fast fixes. These are improvements to our immigration policy that can be made quickly and can benefit all Americans.

All three pillars of immigration reform are important, but strengthening the rule of law is the most critical.

Immigration law is a ubiquitous element in the entire immigration ecosystem. It is needed to process millions of immigration petitions at the National Visa Center and is what informs the decisions of thousands of consular officers around the world.

Immigration law guides the decisions of Customs and Border Protection officers all over America. It allows our courts, including the Supreme Court, to rule on immigration cases. Solid immigration policy makes America stronger.

By plugging the holes in some of our current laws, we can make an impact on the entire legal process—the same process that is used by the majority of immigrants who come to America. It is estimated that 1.5 million immigrants entered the United States in 2016.[8] Eighty percent of them, or 1.2 million, entered the United States legally according to the US Department of State.

The majority of immigrants enter the United States through legal channels. Strengthening our existing legal infrastructure to protect our country is what will net the most value. As I've said, the other pillars are important, but strengthening the law makes the most far-reaching impact.

---

8   Jie Zong, Migration Policy Institute.

Let's compare immigration reform to water damage. You experience a huge water leak at home. Your plumber determines you need comprehensive piping repair throughout your house.

In spite of the appeal of this comprehensive solution, there are practical limitations. This will require a major budget allocation. Not to mention that you will not have any water in your house during the project and must pull local construction permits from the city. This will be time consuming and need extensive approvals.

When taking all these factors into consideration, what would you do? Would you choose to move forward with the comprehensive piping? Or do you fix the existing pipes first? My strategy would be to start with plugging the holes in the existing pipes. Compared to the alternative, this is a cost and time effective solution.

I am aware that this is not the most sustainable long-term answer. But by plugging in the holes, you can retake control of the water situation. You can then take further action on your own terms and schedule. You can increase or decrease the flow of water using the faucets. You can move forward with a more lasting solution.

The same strategy applies to our current immigration situation. There are major holes in current laws that need to be addressed now. Plugging these holes can be done in a timely and cost effective manner. Our policymakers can take rapid control of the immigration situation, and then they can move forward with a more lasting solution.

The onus is not on the immigrant to respect the intent of the law; instead, it is on the US government to ensure the loopholes in the laws are closed. This is what my internship program did after I applied as an African American. Since this was not the intent of the program, they made sure the race categories were further defined. The African American category became "Black or African American." It was defined as a person having origins in any of the black racial groups of Africa. People from the Middle East and North Africa were included in the white category.

The changes made to the race categories were important. The requirements for applying to the program became consistent with the intentions of the directors. We must do the same with our immigration laws. The requirements to come to America must be in line with the intention of the law.

CONCLUSION

Serving the United States as a diplomat was challenging and rewarding. Being a consular officer gave me unique insight into the immigration process. I learned that there are gaps in our immigration laws. Furthermore, the requirements to immigrate to America do not always reflect immigration law. These gaps are not in the interest of the American people.

Knowledgeable foreigners all over the world are exploiting these gaps. We need immigration laws that cannot be manipulated. Americans want to know their government can control the flow of immigrants based on America's needs.

We expect our elected officials to take action in the interest of the United States, but this may be a long time coming. Our lawmakers continue to use the refrain of comprehensive immigration reform. This type of legislation will not happen anytime soon.

Instead, we can take matters into our own hands. We can propose new regulations that enforce our laws in a more pro-American manner. To reach this vision, we need to first understand how people become Americans. In the next chapter, I will provide a general overview of how people do this. Having this foundation is important to understanding the gaps in our immigration policy.

CHAPTER 3

———— ★ ————

AMERICAN APPEAL

INTRODUCTION

If you were born in America, think about how lucky you are. At birth you became an American citizen. You had immediate access to the land of opportunity and the largest economy in the world. The opportunities for your professional growth are only limited by your own imagination. You have the freedom to express yourself in a way that is not possible in most of the world. You have these luxuries because of where you were born.

If you became an American through naturalization, you should also think about how lucky you are. You had a dream to leave a home that you once knew and to make America your new home. Through a family relationship, a job opportunity, or even a little luck, your dream came true.

Millions of people all over the world are hoping to be in your shoes. I spoke to thousands of people who dream of becoming Americans. They imagine pursuing their own version of the American dream, but this possibility is not available to everyone.

There are a few ways to become American. They all involve being born in America, having an American parent, or immigration. For example, my brother became an American citizen because he was born in Boston, and I became an American through immigration.

It is important for you to have an idea of how people become American, and a sense of why people pursue citizenship, in order to identify and close the gaps in American immigration policy.

In this chapter, we will review why foreigners pursue American citizenship. The most popular reason that we hear about is to leave behind a life of poverty. This is true, but it is not the only reason. We will examine others.

Next, we will learn the basics on how people become Americans. This will not be an exhaustive discussion—it will only cover the main ways most people get citizenship. The information provided in this chapter will not make you an expert in US immigration and citizenship, but will give you a solid foundation about the basics.

THE POWER OF AMERICAN CITIZENSHIP

American citizenship is one of the most coveted citizenships in the world. People believe that it is the greatest gift that they can give themselves and their children. As an American citizen, one has the right to live, study, and work in the largest economy in the world. The land of opportunity becomes your land. Let's look at some of the reasons why some foreigners want American citizenship:

INSURANCE

You have the entire weight of the most powerful government on earth behind you as an American. In a world full of conflict and turmoil, American citizenship is the best insurance policy one can have.

Chris Voss, the FBI's former lead international kidnapping negotiator, tells a story that demonstrates this. A twelve-year-old boy was kidnapped with his father in a brutal carjacking in Haiti. It was a Thursday afternoon. The father was released to secure the ransom for his son. For most Haitians, the local Haitian authorities would be their only hope to navigate this situation. But this guy had an insurance policy—his son was born in the United States and was an American citizen.

The father reported the kidnapping to the US embassy in Haiti. He was told that the FBI was going to help him, and, a little while later, he received a call from Voss. Voss oversaw the negotiation strategy of every American kidnapped overseas. He was the best-case scenario to get the kid back. With the FBI's help, the dad had his son back safe and sound by Saturday morning.[9] The kidnapped boy in Haiti had the world's leading kidnapping negotiator on his case, all because of where he was born.

In Lebanon, American citizenship was very important during the 2006 Lebanon War. The US embassy evacuated 15,000 Americans from Lebanon during the war, by air and sea, since they were under the protection of the American government. Many of those evacuated were Lebanese citizens who also had US citizenship. Some had never lived in the US and received temporary documents to travel.

In contrast, Lebanese citizens had to take their chances. They drove to Syria to escape the war. Frightened families packed cars and vans to leave the country. Most of the vehicles had white flags in the windows in hopes that they would be safe from bombardment. But, unlike the Americans, their safety could not be guaranteed. Israeli warplanes leveled roads and bridges throughout the country, making it difficult to drive out of Lebanon.

---

9   Voss, *Never Split the Difference*, 63.

OPPORTUNITY

Foreigners also see American nationality as an opportunity for their children. This is the reason my mother fought to get my brother and me to the United States. With US citizenship, one has the option to live, work, and study here.

By becoming a citizen, foreigners will not have to apply for visas to visit America. They can qualify for scholarships available to American students and apply for any job in the United States. They can apply for jobs in the private sector and don't have to worry about finding a company to sponsor their work visas. They can even apply for federal jobs in the US public sector. In short, US citizenship opens their access to the land of opportunity.

CONVENIENCE

American nationality is convenient. A United States passport is powerful tool for traveling around the world. Most Americans take for granted that they can book a flight, find a place to stay, and travel to most of the world; additionally, they can visit a majority of these countries without even having to get a visa.

For people who do not have this benefit, they must plan their travel well in advance. They must apply for visas for each country they want to travel to. People have missed out on business meetings, academic semesters, and even weddings—all because they could not get their visas. The ability to travel freely is an attractive benefit to people from all over the world to pursue a US passport.

PRESTIGE

The American nationality is prestigious. Holding a US passport is seen as a symbol of social status abroad— people are quick to say they have an American passport in conversations. They can travel anywhere at any time unlike "others." Even if they don't have a US passport, they are just as happy to announce that their child or children hold a US citizenship. It is a badge of honor that shows they were able to "secure the future" for their children.

Even receiving the US embassy's warden message is a point of pride for people who hold US passports abroad. Warden messages are part of the US embassy's outreach to US citizens. Warden messages announce emergencies and distribute information of interest to the American community. This includes demonstrations, areas to exercise caution, and information about a government shutdown. US citizens, or the guardians of US citizens, receive these electronic messages.

In reality, much of this information is available on the

US embassy's or State Department's website. But receiving an email directly from the department gives people a sense of being in the know and a "friend" of the US embassy. This association is a form of social capital among people all over the world.

These are only some of the reasons that millions of people seek to become Americans. Now let's examine how the majority of them become American.

AMERICAN AT BIRTH
BIRTHRIGHT CITIZENSHIP

When I was growing up, I thought it was natural that you became a citizen where you were born. I was born in Egypt, so I was an Egyptian citizen at birth. My brother was born in America, so he was an American citizen at birth. Later, I learned there is more of a distinction. I was born an Egyptian citizen because I was the child of Egyptian parents—not because I was born in Egypt. Being born in Egypt does not make you an Egyptian citizen.

My brother was born an American because he was born in the United States. Being born in the United States makes you an American citizen. This is called birthright citizenship and is a privilege offered by our country.

Birthright citizenship was introduced in 1868. The Fourteenth Amendment to the US Constitution guarantees birthright citizenship. It states that "All persons born or naturalized in the United States, and subject to the jurisdiction thereof, are citizens of the United States and of the State wherein they reside." This means that, if a person is born in the US and is governed by local laws, then he or she is an American citizen at birth.

The intent of the Fourteenth Amendment was to ensure full citizenship to former slaves and their children. It prevented individual states from writing new laws depriving them of their rights. It overrode the Dred Scott decision by the Supreme Court that forbade African Americans from ever gaining citizenship.

The phrase "subject to the jurisdiction thereof" is important. It was intended to exclude from automatic citizenship American-born people who did not have allegiance to the United States. One example of this would be Native American Indians, who, for decades, were excluded from American citizenship because of their tribal law. Since Native American Indians were seen as governed by their tribal jurisdiction, they did not fall under United States jurisdiction. It took decades of legal battles to make citizenship a reality for them. In 1924, Congress granted citizenship to all Native Americans born in the US.

Under the Fourteenth Amendment, the children of foreign diplomats are excluded from birthright citizenship. Foreign diplomats have diplomatic immunity, which excludes them from being subject to local jurisdiction. In other words, this means that foreign diplomats are not subject to lawsuit or prosecution under US laws.

The first time I heard of "diplomatic immunity" was when I was watching the movie *Lethal Weapon 2*. It was in the last action scene of the movie, where South African consul Arjen Rudd shoots police officer Martin Riggs eleven times. Riggs's partner, Roger Murtaugh, orders Rudd to drop his gun. Rudd takes out his diplomatic credentials and shouts out "diplomatic immunity." In true Hollywood fashion, Murtaugh puts a bullet in Rudd's head and says "it's just been revoked." By taking out his diplomatic credentials, Rudd was claiming diplomatic immunity. He was confirming that, as a South African diplomat, he was not subject to local US laws.

Diplomats and their families don't fall under US jurisdiction. Therefore, children of foreign diplomats don't qualify for US citizenship, even if they were born in America. The US-born child of a British diplomat who has been living and working in the US for years will not gain US citizenship. But the child of a nondiplomat who enters the US legally or illegally only to give birth will gain US citizenship.

The United States is very special in offering birthright citizenship. There are only thirty countries in the world that offer this privilege. Of the top ten economies in the world, only the United States, Brazil, and Canada offer birthright citizenship. Children born to foreign parents in China, France, Germany, India, and the United Kingdom do not become citizens of those countries. We will examine birthright citizenship in more detail in chapter 4.

BORN TO AMERICAN PARENTS

If a child is born outside the United States, they are not entitled to birthright citizenship. However, they can acquire US citizenship through an American citizen parent—which includes an adoptive parent. The law requires that the American parent who is passing on their citizenship must have lived in the US for a period of time specified by Congress. The child also has to be less than eighteen years old and not married in order to gain citizenship.

For example, Robert was born in France eight years ago. His mother is an American citizen who moved to France after college because she fell in love with Paris. Robert is entitled to US citizenship because his mother is American and she lived in the United States.

On the other hand, Martine was born in Canada. Her

father is an American citizen because he was born in the US, but he never lived in America. Therefore, Martine is not entitled to US citizenship because of this.

AMERICAN BY NATURALIZATION

STEP ONE: IMMIGRATION VISA

People who are not American by birth may become naturalized American citizens. Naturalization is the process by which a person acquires citizenship of a country. For naturalized American citizens, the process usually begins with an immigrant visa (IV). IVs are issued at US embassies and consulates around the world. They allow the applicant, their spouse, and any qualifying children to immigrate to the US.

There are several ways to get an immigrant visa. We will look at the most popular types of IVs. The following table is a summary of immigrant visas issued during the period 2014–18.

	2014	2015	2016	2017	2018	Total
Family-Based	382,890	452,272	530,850	466,585	448,167	2,280,764
Diversity Visas	51,018	48,097	45,664	49,067	48,578	242,424
Employment-Based	21,365	21,613	25,056	23,814	27,345	119,193
Special Immigrants	12,097	9,481	16,182	20,070	9,467	67,297
Total Immigrant	455,273	521,982	601,570	539,466	524,090	2,642,381

Table 1: Immigrant Visas issued by US Consulate 2014–18

Family-Based Immigrant Visas

The most common types of IVs are family-based immigrant visas. These are immigrant visas based on a familial relationship with a US citizen or green card holder. The US citizen or green card holder must fill out an application. This application is an official request for an immigrant visa for their foreign relative. This is called the petitioning process—the application is called the petition, and the US citizen or green card holder is the petitioner.

From 2014 to 2018, almost 2.7 million immigrant visas were issued at US consulates all over the world. Eighty-four percent of those were to family members of the US citizens and permanent residents. The United States has a policy of putting families first when it comes to immigration.

Not all family members of US citizens and green card

holders can qualify for immigrant visas, though. There are two family-based immigration visa categories: immediate relatives (IR) and family preference (FP).

Immediate relatives are spouses, unmarried children under twenty-one, adopted children, and parents of American citizens. There is no annual limit on the number of immediate relative visas that may be issued by the State Department. This means consular officers all over the world can issue as many of them as needed.

The family preference category is for US citizens' married and unmarried children over twenty-one years old. It is also for spouses, children under twenty-one years of age, and unmarried sons and daughters (age twenty-one and over) of green card holders. There are limits placed on the number of family preference visas that may be issued each year. For example, in 2018, there were only 23,400 immigrant visas for unmarried sons and daughters of US citizens that are over twenty-one.

To summarize, the difference between the two categories is that immediate relative visas are only for relatives of US citizens, and there are no limits on the number of these that can be issued. In contrast, family preference visas are for relatives of both US citizens and green card holders, and there are limits on the number of these that can be issued.

This means that the waiting time to receive an immigrant visa in the family preference category is longer than the immediate relative category. The Consul's Corner at the end of this chapter provides a summary of family-based immigration visa categories.

There are millions of people who want to come to the US legally with immigrant visas. The number of qualified applicants always exceeds the number of available visas. Millions of people must wait years, or even decades, to have their immigrant visas processed.

For example, as of January 2019, if you were a twenty-nine-year-old married Jordanian daughter of a US citizen who had applied for an immigrant visa in February 2007, you would still be waiting for your application to be processed. That is a wait of over eleven years. Similarly, if you were a thirty-five-year-old unmarried Mexican son of a US green card holder who had applied for an immigrant visa in October 1997, you would still be waiting for your visa to be processed. That is a wait of over twenty-one years. We will look at family-based immigrant visas in more detail in chapter 5.

Employment-Based Immigrant Visas

Foreigners may also receive immigrant visas based on employment. In this situation, an American company needs the skills of a foreign worker and petitions for that individual to come and work with it. In order for this to be successful, the foreign worker should have extraordinary abilities in sciences, business, arts, or sports.

For example, the EB-1 immigrant visa is for exceptional ability. It is referred to as the "Einstein visa." This is because Albert Einstein immigrated to America—he did so by accepting the position of professor of theoretical physics at Princeton University. Wayne Rooney, a professional soccer player from the United Kingdom, also came to America on an employment-based visa. He plays for the Major League Soccer (MLS) club D.C. United. Rooney is able to work for MLS by using an employment-based visa.

Technology companies from California to Boston all rely on foreign employees. Tech companies believe foreign employees make them more competitive. As of 2017, 57 percent of the San Francisco Bay Area's tech workforce was born outside of the US.[10] Most of these foreign workers come to the US on employment-based visas.

Employment-based immigration visa applications need a labor certification, which must be approved by the US Department of Labor. This is to protect American workers—it certifies that foreign workers are not taking jobs

10 Melville, "Silicon Valley Competitiveness and Innovation Project."

from qualified workers who are citizens. If the Department of Labor finds that qualified American workers are available, then it denies the labor certificate as well as the foreign worker's visa application.

Diversity-Based Immigrant Visas

The diversity-based immigrant visa (DV) is a popular type of immigrant visa. People all over the world call it "the green card lottery." The DV's purpose is to expand the countries where immigrants come from, and there are only 50,000 available every year. Only people born in countries with low rates of immigration to the US can apply for the diversity visa. A low rate of immigration is less than 50,000 immigrants to the US in the previous five years. Some countries with low rates of immigration to the US include Thailand, Kuwait, Ethiopia, Finland, New Zealand, and Chile.

Diversity visa applicants are not required to have a petitioner. This is different than other types of immigrant visas—a foreigner can just simply apply. If selected, they receive the diversity visa and can immigrate to the US within six months. We will look at diversity visas in more detail in chapter 7.

STEP TWO: FROM IMMIGRANT VISA TO GREEN CARD

After arriving in the US on an immigrant visa, the immigrant may apply for their legal permanent residency card, or green card. Immigrant visas are issued at US consulates abroad, but it is the US Citizenship and Immigration Services, located in the United States, that issues green cards.

The time required to receive the green card varies based on the type of immigrant visa acquired. For example, it is usually faster to receive a green card from family-based immigration than employment-based immigration. The green card identifies the person as a legal resident in the US but not yet an American citizen.

To maintain a green card, the immigrant cannot be outside the US for more than twelve months at a time. They must also not have the intention to permanently move to another country. This means that for an immigrant to keep their green card, they need to make sure that they don't spend more than a year outside the US at any one time. They must ensure that their intention is to live in America, but they don't actually have to be permanently and physically living there throughout the year.

STEP THREE: FROM GREEN CARD TO NATURALIZATION CERTIFICATE (CITIZENSHIP)

The final step in the naturalization process is to apply for American citizenship. This comes after fulfilling requirements as a legal permanent resident. The applicant must fulfill "continuous residence" and "physical presence" requirements. Most immigrants must prove five years of continuous residency in America.[11] This means the immigrant must have a permanent home in America. They cannot be away from this home for more than six months at any one time during the five years.

The immigrant must also prove that they were physically present in the US for at least half of the continuous residence. That means that they were physically living in the US for thirty out of sixty months.

For example, Thomas has been a green card holder for the past five years. He travels back to Ecuador, where he was born, every few months. He has never been outside the US for more than six months at a time, yet he was only physically present there for twenty-four of the past sixty months. Thomas' green card continues to be valid, but he is not allowed to apply for US citizenship. He can only apply for citizenship once he spends thirty out of sixty months in America. We will look at the naturalization process in more detail in chapter 8.

---

11   For spouses of US citizens, less time is required.

BECOMING AN AMERICAN SUMMARY

In a nutshell, there are limited ways to become a US citizen. You can be born here, born to an American parent, or become a naturalized US citizen.

Most people who become naturalized US citizens do so by first getting an immigrant visa at one of our consulates abroad. The immigrant visa can be based on a family relationship, employment, or diversity. After arriving in the US with the immigrant visa, the person can apply for a green card.

The green card holder can qualify to apply for US citizenship after completing all continuous residency and physical presence requirements. The following is a summary of the process we discussed:

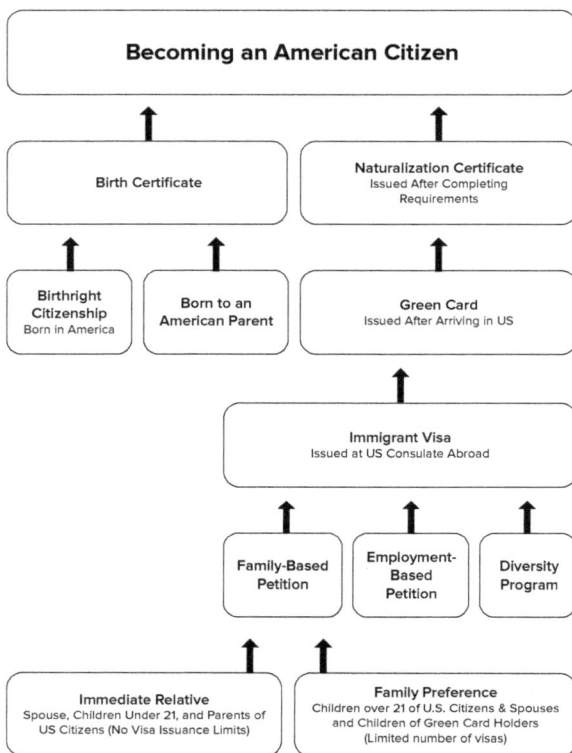

Becoming an American Citizen

Birth Certificate

Naturalization Certificate
Issued After Completing Requirements

Birthright Citizenship
Born in America

Born to an American Parent

Green Card
Issued After Arriving in US

Immigrant Visa
Issued at US Consulate Abroad

Family-Based Petition

Employment-Based Petition

Diversity Program

Immediate Relative
Spouse, Children Under 21, and Parents of US Citizens (No Visa Issuance Limits)

Family Preference
Children over 21 of U.S. Citizens & Spouses and Children of Green Card Holders (Limited number of visas)

*Not a Comprehensive List

Figure 1: Becoming an American Citizen

CONCLUSION

The day I became an America citizen was one of the most significant days of my life. It was the day that a world of opportunities became available to me. It was the day that the son of a single mother on welfare could become a US diplomat.

I do not take this day for granted because I know it is not available to everyone. A lucky few are born in America or are the children of American parents. For others, the road is harder to become a naturalized American. In both cases, the process to become American is fraught with gaps—ones that some immigrants are exploiting.

Now, let's learn about five of these gaps and look at the ways in which we can fix them. In the next chapter, we will examine the gaps in birthright citizenship. We will also look at how people use tourist visas to give birth to their children in America so their kids receive citizenship.

THE CONSUL'S CORNER: FAMILY-BASED IMMIGRANT VISA CATEGORIES

Immediate Relative Immigrant Visas (Unlimited): Based on a close family relationship with a US citizen. The number of visas issued in this category is not limited each year. Immediate relative visa types include the following:

- IR-1: Spouse of a US Citizen

- IR-2: Unmarried Child Under 21 Years of Age of a US Citizen

- IR-3: Orphan adopted abroad by a US Citizen

- IR-4: Orphan to be adopted in the US by a US citizen

- IR-5: Parent of a US Citizen who is at least 21 years old

Family Preference Immigrant Visas (Limited): For distant, family relationships with a US citizen and some relationships with green card holders. There limits on the number of family preference visas that may be issued. The family preference types and the approximate number of visas allocated for each type in the 2018–19 fiscal year are

- Family First Preference (F1): Unmarried sons and daughters of US citizens, and their minor children, if any. (23,400)

- Family Second Preference A (F2A): Spouses and minor children of green card holders. (88,000)

- Family Second Preference B (F2B): Unmarried sons and daughters (age twenty-one and over) of green card holders. (26,200)

- Family Third Preference (F3): Married sons and daughters of US citizens, and their spouses and minor children. (23,400)

- Family Fourth Preference (F4): Brothers and sisters of US citizens, and their spouses and minor children, provided the US citizens are at least twenty-one years of age. (65,000)

The amount of time an applicant must wait to receive their visas will vary from months to decades depending on the category and the type. The family preference category has a longer wait time than the immediate relative category.

*Data provided by the US Department of State—Bureau of Consular Affairs

https://travel.state.gov/content/travel/en/us-visas/immigrate/family-immigration/family-based-immigrant-visas.html#1

CHAPTER 4

---- ★ ----

BIRTHRIGHT CITIZENSHIP

INTRODUCTION

"So-called Birthright Citizenship, which costs our country billions of dollars and is very unfair to our citizens, will be ended one way or the other. It is not covered by the 14th Amendment because of the words 'subject to the jurisdiction thereof.'" With this tweet, President Trump put birthright citizenship back in the political spotlight.

Birthright citizenship means becoming a citizen of a country by being born in its territory. As I have explained, the United States offers birthright citizenship. It has been a topic of fierce debate for decades. Some people feel that birthright citizenship is part of what makes America special, while others think that the birthright citizenship law is being abused.

People come to the US, legally and illegally, to give birth to their children. They want their kids to have American citizenship and the benefits that we reviewed in chapter 3. But, clearly, their actions are not in line with the intention of the law.

Ending birthright citizenship, as President Trump wants to do, would not be easy. It requires a Supreme Court ruling and clarification to the Constitution. While possible, this would be very time consuming.

In this chapter, I provide an alternative to ending birthright citizenship. We will explore how we can discourage foreigners from abusing the privilege. I recommend that foreign mothers and fathers of children who are born in the US using tourist visas not receive tourist visas in the future. They can't attend business meetings, medical treatment, or social functions in America. Refusing tourist visas to foreign parents who exploited birthright citizenship will discourage others from doing the same.

I recognize that this will not end birthright tourism. But it will deter some of the 40,000 mothers who come to the US each year only to give birth and receive citizenship for their child. It will also send a message—that the United States is keen on closing the gaps in its immigration policies.

BIRTHRIGHT TOURISM

Birthright citizenship is a contentious issue in our country. Many feel that birthright citizenship is part of America's identity. But there are also many who feel that offering US citizenship to people who come to our country only to give birth is a manipulation of the law.

When we think of women who come to America to give birth, we usually think of illegal immigrants. We imagine mothers taking painful journeys—coyotes smuggle them into the United States, and they give birth in horrifying circumstances. This is all done so that the newborn child will automatically become an American citizen, and the parents can then use the baby to remain here. This is why these kids are called "anchor babies."[12]

The issue of American-born children of illegal immigrants is important. It needs attention—but these are not the cases that I am focusing on. Instead, my focus is on women who enter the United States, legally, to give birth to their children.

These women usually enter on tourist visas—we call this birthright tourism. The Center for Immigration Studies estimates that 40,000 babies are born each year using birthright tourism. Women travel to the US using valid visas to have babies and, after having their children, they

---

12   Some people consider the term anchor baby derogatory.

leave the United States as required with their new American citizen. The Consul's Corner summarizes how people can become US citizens.

Our current policy does not prohibit pregnant women from traveling to America, nor does it prevent women from giving birth in America. Let's look at how it is legally possible for women to travel to America to give birth:

GIVING BIRTH ON TOURIST VISAS

Most people that come to America on temporary visits do so on tourist visas (B visa). The tourist visa may be used for short-term visits to the US for business, medical, and tourism purposes. These visas are issued at US consulates abroad.

A foreign woman may apply for a tourist visa to have medical treatment, including giving birth. The applicant must provide a medical diagnosis from a local physician. It should explain the reason for the treatment in the United States. The applicant also needs a letter from a physician or medical facility in the United States. It should express a willingness to treat this specific ailment as well as include the projected length of time and cost of the treatment. The applicant also has to provide evidence of their ability to pay for the treatment. The consular officer will review all these documents, and it is up to them to determine if the applicant qualifies.

Expecting parents may also travel using previously issued visas. This is because visas may be given for longer periods of time than the length of the trip the visa was originally for. The time between the date the visa is issued, or given, and the date that it expires is called the visa validity. Depending on the applicant's nationality, visas can be valid for many years. For example, Chinese and Indian citizens can be issued a visa with a validity of up to ten years. An Ecuadorian can be issued a visa with a validity of up to five years. Visas may also be issued for single entry or multiple/unlimited entries.

For example, Nancy is from Ukraine. She applied for a tourist visa to attend an engineering conference in Chicago in July 2019. Her visa was issued in June 2019 and is valid until June 2029. This is because Ukrainians can have tourist visas with a validity of up to ten years. Nancy travels to the US for two weeks as scheduled to attend her conference. She can then continue to use the same visa until June 2029 in order to travel to America for short-term visits without going back to the US consulate.

GIVING BIRTH ON ELECTRONIC SYSTEM FOR TRAVEL AUTHORIZATION (ESTA)

There are other women who can travel to give birth in the US without a visa. There are thirty-eight nationalities around the world that qualify for the visa waiver program (VWP). The program allows most citizens of VWP countries to travel to the United States for touristic visits for up to ninety days—without needing a visa from a US consulate to do so. These travelers must meet certain requirements—they must have an electronic passport that is valid for at least six months and, also, not be associated with any of the countries listed under the Terrorist Travel Prevention Act.[13]

By meeting these requirements, they can travel to the US using the Electronic System for Travel Authorization (ESTA). The traveler can fill out the ESTA application online. All they need is a credit card to pay the fee—there is no interview with a consular officer. With an approved ESTA, they can travel to the US for up to ninety days for business, tourism, or medical purposes.

In the following section, we will look at a typical case of parents using birthright tourism. They use our own

---

13 On January 21, 2016, the United States began implementing changes under the Visa Waiver Program Improvement and Terrorist Travel Prevention Act of 2015. Nationals of VWP countries who have traveled to, or been present in, Iraq, Iran, Libya, Somalia, Sudan, Syria, and/or Yemen on or after March 1, 2011, are no longer eligible to travel or be admitted to the United States under the VWP.

laws to get American citizenship for their children. Pay attention—because you will be asked to be the consular officer later in the chapter.

MEET MARIAM

Mariam is a married Egyptian business-outsourcing consultant. At the age of thirty, Mariam applied for a tourist visa to attend a business meeting in the United States. After her interview with the consular officer, she was issued a five-year, multiple-entry visa. This means that she can travel to the US until she is thirty-five years old.

At the age of thirty-two, Mariam becomes pregnant. She decides that she wants to give birth to her child in America. She believes the hospitals are safer in the US than Egypt. More importantly, if she gives birth in the US, her child will also get American citizenship. She could always give birth in the UK or France. These countries are closer to Egypt, and they have good hospitals as well. But they do not offer birthright citizenship—it makes more sense for Mariam to take advantage of the opportunity that the US is providing.

Since Mariam still has a full-validity tourist visa, she can travel to the US without having to apply for a new one. That makes things easier for her. She arrives at Tucson International Airport about two months before her delivery date. She travels with her mom for moral support as her husband can't take two months off of work to be with her. He may travel to the US closer to the delivery date. She has a friend who lives in Tucson, so it will be a good opportunity to catch up with her. Mariam rents a two-bedroom apartment for a reasonable price for three months. She is planning to remain in the US for a month after the delivery for any needed follow-up.

A border control officer from the Department of Homeland Security (DHS) greets her. He checks her visa and asks her questions. He will decide whether to allow her to enter the US and for how long she can stay. He asks her questions to determine the date the child is due for delivery. He wants to know the length of time she intends to stay in America. He also wants evidence that she has medical insurance for all medical necessities.

She is able to prove that she has enough medical insurance to cover any complications. She is also able to prove that her reason for coming to the US is legitimate. She is also able to show that she can afford her visit. There is no law prohibiting her from entering the US while pregnant, so the immigration officer allows her entry.

Over the next few weeks, Mariam and her mother shop for everything the baby will need. She knows it will be a boy and purchases clothes, a stroller, bottles, etc. Weeks later, Mariam gives birth to a baby boy that she names Sheriff. She receives his birth certificate demonstrating he was born in America and, therefore, is an American citizen. She immediately applies for his American passport. Once she receives the baby's passport, she travels back to Egypt as scheduled.

The trip cost Mariam approximately $25,000. She paid for airfare tickets, hospital expenses, and living expenses. The child's passport cost $115. Receiving American citizenship from the US government was free. Mariam effectively purchased a US citizenship for her new son with all the advantages that come with it.

Mariam is not alone—she joins a group of hundreds of thousands of women. Every year, approximately 40,000 women travel to the US to give birth for birthright citizenship. She has not done anything illegal. Much like Ty Montgomery of the Packers, she used the existing rules to her, and her child's, advantage.

THE GAP IN BIRTHRIGHT CITIZENSHIP

Giving birth in the US for birthright citizenship may not be illegal, but it is not the intention of the law. The intent of the Fourteenth Amendment in 1868 was to ensure citizenship for slaves and their children—not to allow birthright tourism. Still, each year, tens of thousands of women board airplanes to America, give birth, receive citizenship for their children, and leave.

People all over the world may not know the intention of the Fourteenth Amendment. But they can reason that its purpose is not for foreigners to come to America and give birth. They assume that because this is not the intention of the law, it is likely not legal. I know this because of my time as a consul—women almost never tell consular officers they want to give birth in America in an interview.

I conducted thousands of visa interviews as a consular officer. Not once did a woman declare giving birth as the reason for her travel. Instead, most applicants who had this intention misrepresented the purposes of their visits. They claimed to be visiting friends and family. They wanted to attend conferences. They even wanted to visit Disneyland. But it was never because they wanted to give birth in America.

Women came to interviews wearing loose clothing to hide their pregnancies. Some even wore tight support braces around their midriffs to minimize how much their pregnancies showed. Other applicants denied they were pregnant at all.

One woman stands out in my mind. It was a hot day in June, and I could barely stand having my tie on as I walked from my home to the consulate. A woman came to my interview window with a trench coat on. There were only two reasons to wear a trench coat on that day—either she hated air conditioning or she was trying to cover up a pregnancy.

As we started the interview, she told me that the purpose of her travel was to visit her sister. I smiled and confided to her that I hated air conditioning. I asked her, "Are you wearing a coat because you are like me and hate the AC, or is there another reason? And, before you answer, be very careful. Your response at this moment will determine your qualification for a visa for many years to come." She understood the gravity of the situation. She admitted that she was pregnant and that she was considering giving birth in America. I refused her visa.

The refusal was not because she was going to give birth in America. This is not a basis for refusal because it is not illegal. She was refused because she could not prove the financial ability to cover the delivery in America. At least by telling me the truth she did not have the dreaded "lied to a consular officer" on her record. If she was marked with that phrase, it is possible she would never be issued a tourist visa in the future.

The problem is that, even when people act outside the intention of the Fourteenth Amendment, there are no consequences. Parents take advantage of birthright citizenship and give birth in the US with a tourist visa—and continue to qualify for more tourist visas. Think about that—someone who gamed the system is only rewarded.

Just like the Packers, who were given a start at the forty-yard line, these parents are gifted with further travel to America. One woman, who provided information for this book, gave birth to two children using one tourist visa. She was later issued another tourist visa and used it to give birth to a third child in our country. Her three children are all American citizens, and they have never lived in America.

CLOSING THE GAP: DENY TOURIST VISAS TO PARENTS

There are a few ways to close the gap in birthright tourism. The first is to deny citizenship to babies born to foreign parents. This option requires a clear explanation of the phrase "subject to the jurisdiction thereof."

We need to know if foreigners who temporarily come to the US are subject to our country's jurisdiction. If not, then their children should not be US citizens—just like the children of diplomats. This was the point President Trump was making in his tweet. He thinks birthright citizenship does not apply to foreigners since they are not subject to US jurisdiction.

YOU BE THE CONSUL

Now it's time for you to be the consul. Imagine that you are a consular officer at the US embassy in the Philippines. You are sitting in a high chair and desk behind bulletproof glass. Dividers separate your workspace from other consular officers. There is a microphone that allows you to talk with the applicants on the other side of the interview window. The waiting area is full of applicants hoping to get a visa to the US. You call the next applicant to your window. "Jasmine Mahalia, window number four," you say into the speaker.

Jasmine is a citizen of the Philippines. She wants to travel to the US for a medical conference and then visit the Grand Canyon. She intends to travel in two weeks and will stay in the US for three weeks.

She is a dentist in the Philippines, and her husband is a businessman. She has traveled to the US several times before and has the money to pay for her trip. She qualifies for a tourist visa to attend the conference and visit the Grand Canyon.

In the Philippines, a tourist visa can have a visa validity of five years. Would you give her a full-validity, multiple-entry visa? The answer is probably yes because she has traveled to the US several times before and had a good tourist profile.

Is it possible that Jasmine will use that visa in the future to give birth in America? Although that is not the reason given when you issued the visa, it is certainly possible.

By issuing the full-validity, multiple-entry visa, you acted under our current rules. But you may have also inadvertently participated in exploiting birthright citizenship.

This is Donald Trump's opinion, but others disagree. There has been debate on this issue for decades. Clarifying birthright citizenship laws could require a Supreme Court decision. It could also need a Constitutional amendment. This would be time consuming and not practical in the current political atmosphere. In the meantime, nothing prevents foreign parents from continuing to exploit birthright citizenship laws.

I want to discourage parents from giving birth in the US on tourist visas. To do so, I recommend proposing a new regulation to the Department of State. It would require consular officers to deny tourist visas to parents who gave birth in the US on a prior tourist visa. To determine the practicality of this recommendation, we need to understand how consular officers make decisions on tourist visas.

LEGAL BASIS

The Immigration and Nationality Act (INA) guides decisions on tourist visas. Law 214(b) requires consular officers to assume that all tourist visa applicants are intended immigrants. The consular officer must assume the tourist visa applicant wants to use the visa to live in America. Living in the US on a tourist visa is against the law.

The applicant must prove that they are not intending to

immigrate to America. They must show the consular officer that they have strong ties to their country. These ties will compel then to leave the United States at the end of their visit; otherwise, the consular officer refuses the visa.

Ties are the various aspects of the applicant's life that binds them to their country. Strong ties vary from applicant to applicant. While conducting visa interviews, the officers will look at each application individually. The officer will consider the applicant's work history and home situation. He or she will consider family ties, travel plans, and financial resources. Based on these factors, the officer determines the applicant's intent under the law.

During my time as a consul, I interviewed thousands of nonimmigrant visa applicants. I had to assume the applicant wanted to use the visa to immigrate to America. It did not matter if they were eight or eighty, male or female, a doctor or a doorman. It was up to the applicant to show me that they had enough ties to their country to return after a short stay in America. If not, I had to refuse the visa.

For example, a young man who I interviewed for a tourist visa wanted to go to Las Vegas. I asked about the purpose of his trip, which made him blush and look behind him in a sheepish way to see if anyone could hear what he was saying. At many US consulates, the interview room is a large open space with no real privacy. He looked at me and whispered, "You know, Las Vegas stuff."

I could not help but smile. I appreciated his honesty. As we talked, I found out that he had recently finished university and did not yet have a regular, full-time job. He lived with his parents and never traveled outside his country before. He had a girlfriend for the past two years who was still at university.

I wanted to give him a visa to go to Las Vegas and do whatever "Las Vegas stuff" he wanted. Unfortunately, he did not have strong ties to his country. He had no job or travel history. In conclusion, he had no tangible reason to come back to his country. He could not overcome my assumption of him being an intending immigrant, and I had no choice but to refuse his tourist visa request.

In another example, a gentleman and his wife came to apply for a tourist visa. He was a retired public sector employee. He and his family received several US visas in the past. During our interview, I learned that, in the past three years, he had spent between six and nine months in the US each year.

He spent so much time in the US because he wanted to visit with his son who was living in America. I could understand his reason for spending so much time in the

US on a sentimental level. But the fact that he spent this amount of time in America indicated to me that he did not have strong ties to his country. He did not qualify for a tourist visa—I refused the visa applications for both him and his wife.

The same logic should apply to mothers and fathers of children who are born in America using a tourist visa—they should not receive further tourist visas. The parents purposefully had a child in America. They took a tangible action to establishing a strong connection with our country. As a parent (imagine being a parent if you are not one), would your attachment to your job, your home, or anything else be more important than the bond to your child? The answer is almost certainly not.

So the tourist visa applicant's strongest tie, or most important element in their life, is a US citizen. Having an American child through birthright citizenship supports the assumption that the parents are intending to immigrate to America. They cannot overcome the assumption of immigrant intent. As mandated by INA 214(b), they should be refused tourist visas.

IMPLEMENTATION

Implementing this new rule is feasible. It will not cost billions of dollars or require changes to the current law. The following is a summary of steps required to implement this recommendation:

Step one: The Department of State issues a policy memorandum to consular officers at US embassies. It explains that parents who gave birth in the US using a tourist visa created strong ties with America. This disqualifies them from receiving further tourist visas. Consular officers should deny tourist visas to applicants who participated in birthright tourism. This guidance is a strict interpretation of law INA 214(b).

There is a precedent for using policy memos in the US government. On July 12, 2018, USCIS issued a policy memorandum (PM-602-0163) to its officers. It stated that they have the discretion to deny an incomplete immigration application. The officer no longer had to follow up with applicants whose applications were not complete.

Before this policy memo, USCIS officers had to accept all immigration applications. If the application was not complete, they had to follow up with the applicants. The officer had to collect missing documents and correct wrong information. There was only limited responsibility on the applicant.

The policy memo put the responsibility on the applicant—USCIS became stricter in its review of cases. If the application is not complete, the USCIS officer can immediately deny it.

The policy memo was not popular among applicants—it was called harsh and unfair. Applicants would need to start the application process all over again if they made a mistake. But USCIS officers reported that the quality of applications improved. After the policy memo, the majority of applications were accurate and complete. USCIS officers could use their time more effectively. This is of benefit to both USCIS and the American taxpayer.

Step two: The State Department needs to know who participated in birthright tourism. This is an easy step to implement. The tourist visa application form (DS-160) already requires information about American relatives. Applicants must list any immediate family members that are US citizens. No new questions are needed on the application—the officer can immediately know if the applicant has a child who is an American citizen.

Step three: Apply the same guidance to visa waiver program (VWP) applicants. Currently, applicants from visa waiver countries submit the ESTA application online. If the application is approved, the applicant can come to the US without an interview. If the ESTA application is denied, the applicant cannot travel to America. Instead, they may go to the local US consulate to apply for a visa.

The ESTA application must be amended. Any applicant who has children who are US citizens should not receive the ESTA. Instead, they would need to go to the local US consulate for a visa interview. The State Department has made this type of amendment before, in January 2016, after the terrorist attacks in Paris. It only affected applicants with ties to Iraq, Iran, Libya, Somalia, Sudan, Syria, or Yemen. They could no longer receive an ESTA and needed a visa to travel to America.

If the applicant indicates ties with these countries, the ESTA application is denied. The applicant is informed that they must appear for an interview with a consular officer. They then apply for a visa like other applicants. At the embassy, the consular officer determines if the applicant can have a visa or not. The decision is based on these new regulations.

The State Department can make the same type of change for birthright tourists. The ESTA will be denied if the applicant indicates that they have an American citizen child by birthright citizenship. They can still apply for a tourist visa, but they will be informed that they must appear for an interview with a consular officer. At the interview, the officer will determine if the new rules apply to the applicant. The visa will be issued or denied accordingly.

A COMMON GROUND

This recommendation is reasonable; it is common ground in the birthright citizenship debate. It requires a new rule and not a new law—which makes it easier to put in place than trying to get a decision by the Supreme Court or to amend the Constitution.

It supports the legal infrastructure that currently exists as well. Consular officers can continue to use law INA 214(b) to decide on tourist visa applications. The Fourteenth Amendment will still be the law of the land.

The US will show that there are consequences to not acting within the intention of the law. People can still come to the US to give birth since it is legal. The child will still have American citizenship since it is the current law. But, since using a tourist visa to give birth and get birthright citizenship is not the intention of the law, there will be consequences.

Parents will not qualify for future tourist visas. They cannot attend business meetings or seek medical attention in America. They will not be able to visit family and friends or take part in other touristic travel. This is a more serious trade-off for giving birth in the US on a tourist visa than what exists today. Foreigners don't mind paying the expenses to give birth in the US if it means that their child receives US citizenship. But having both parents denied from receiving future tourist visas could be too high a price to pay.

Finally, this recommendation can be implemented quickly. It does not conflict with any plans to pursue further legislation on this issue.

CONCLUSION

People should not be rewarded for acting outside the intention of the law. We need a new rule that denies tourist visas to parents who participated in birthright tourism. This is not a comprehensive solution to the abuse of birthright citizenship, but it is a start. It discourages birthright tourism while upholding the Fourteenth Amendment. It is a reasonable common ground in the debate about birthright citizenship. It moves us towards a more pro-American immigration policy.

In this chapter, we looked at a loophole in becoming American—that is, being born in the United States. In the next chapter, we will shift our attention to the naturalization process. We will review the financial requirements for immigrants to come to America. There, we will find yet another loophole—between the financial requirements to bring an immigrant to America and immigration law.

THE CONSUL'S CORNER:
ACQUIRING US CITIZENSHIP

US citizenship may be acquired either by birth or through naturalization.

Birthright Citizenship: Gaining US citizenship is by being born in the United States. To benefit from birthright citizenship the applicant must

- Have been born in the United States or certain territories or outlying possessions of the United States and subject to the jurisdiction of the United States.

- American Parents: There are two ways to obtain citizenship through US citizen parents: at birth, and after birth but before the age of eighteen. Congress has enacted laws that determine how citizenship is conveyed by a US citizen parent (or parents) to children born outside of the United States.

- The law in effect at the time of birth determines whether someone born outside the United States to a US citizen parent (or parents) is a US citizen at birth. In general, these laws require that at least one parent was a US citizen and that the US citizen parent had lived in the United States for a period of time.

- Children born outside the United States may become US citizens after birth by fulfilling all legibility requirements.

Naturalization Process: Naturalization is the process to grant US citizenship to an immigrant after he or she fulfills the requirements established by Congress in the Immigration and Nationality Act (INA). Qualifications include the following:

- Lawful permanent residency for at least five years

and meet all other eligibility requirements.

- Lawful permanent residency for three years or more and meet all eligibility requirements to file as a spouse of a US citizen.

- Qualifying service in the US armed forces and meet all other eligibility requirements.

Data provided by US Citizenship and Naturalization Services:

https://travel.state.gov/content/travel/en/legal/travel-legal-considerations/us-citizenship.html

CHAPTER 5

---- ★ ----

FINANCIAL SPONSORSHIP OF IMMIGRANT VISAS

INTRODUCTION

I'll admit it—I am a link in a chain of migration. Chain migration is alive and well, and I am one of the culprits. My chain consists of my father, mother, grandmother, uncle, aunt, uncle's wife, cousins, granduncle, grandaunt, and more. Like any chain migration family, we started as one and became many. One migrant from Egypt resulted in many immigrants in various parts of the United States.

"Chain migration" is another one of those catchy but contentious phrases being used in the immigration debate. Senator Chris Murphy (D-CT) tweeted that to use the term chain migration "dehumanizes immigrants." "If you're using that word, you're declaring a side," he said. I consider the phrase chain migration to be more descriptive than pejorative. I am not apologetic for being a product of chain migration—it is United States policy that allows its citizens, and permanent residents, to bring family members to America.

The State Department refers to the process as "family-based immigration." Family-based immigration is the legal process to bring foreign family members to America. US citizens and green card holders can use family-based immigration.

A critical part of the family-based immigration is the financial sponsor. The financial sponsor is an American citizen or legal permanent resident. They are financially responsible for the immigrant and must ensure that the immigrant does not become a public charge. That is, they cannot be dependent on US taxpayer help.

As I am writing this book, there is plenty of discussion about public charge. The Trump administration is enforcing rules to discourage foreigners from using public assistance programs in America. As always, there are Americans who support and oppose the administration's actions.

One of the problems is that the financial sponsorship requirements are not consistent with the law. In this chapter, we will examine the gap between financial sponsorship requirements and the law. There are people who sponsor an immigrant application and still qualify for welfare. This is not consistent—either the requirements or the law needs to change.

I recommend a new rule to increase the minimum annual income requirements to sponsor an immigrant. This eliminates the inconsistency—it would prevent a person from sponsoring an immigrant while qualifying for public help. A person should not be able to do both, per our law.

FAMILY-BASED IMMIGRATION REQUIREMENTS

The majority of people who immigrate to America use family-based immigration. During the period 2014–2018, 84 percent of all immigrants were family-based. The application process for a family-based immigrant visa consists of the following:

- A petition (application) from a US citizen or green card holder that has a qualifying relationship with the potential immigrant
- A financial sponsorship by someone in the US (usually but not always the petitioner)
- A medical clearance

- A security clearance
- Confirmation that the applicant is qualified to immigrate to the US after an interview with the consular officer

FINANCIAL SPONSORSHIP

Financial sponsorship is a critical part of immigration law. Congress requires that a financial sponsor sign an affidavit of support. This is for family-based immigrants and is outlined under law INA 213(a).

The financial sponsor must be a US citizen or permanent resident. They take the responsibility to financially support the immigrant, their spouse, and any children. The financial sponsor is usually the petitioner, but it could also be someone else who is willing to take on the responsibility.

A financial sponsor is needed because immigration law requires that an immigrant does not become a "pubic charge." In other words, they cannot be dependent on public assistance from American taxpayers. US immigration law states that immigrants "who, in the opinion of the Consular Officer at the time of application for a visa, or in the opinion of the Attorney General at the time of application for admission or adjustment of status, is likely at any time to become a public charge [are] inadmissible"

(INA 212 (a)(4)). If an immigrant cannot prove they will not depend on public assistance, their visa application must be refused.

The financial sponsor is there to ensure that the immigrant does not become a public charge. Law 8 USC 1601 makes financial sponsorship legal. It states, "It continues to be the immigration policy of the United States that aliens within the Nation's borders not depend on public resources to meet their needs, but rather rely on their own capabilities and the resources of their families, their sponsors, and private organizations."

To qualify as a financial sponsor, the person must show that their income is at least 125 percent of the US poverty level.[14] This requirement depends on the household size as the Department of Health and Human Services (HHS) determines the poverty level. The household size consists of the sponsor and the sponsor's dependents. It also includes relatives living with the sponsor and the immigrant(s) who are being sponsored. The following table provides the fiscal year 2018–2019 HHS US poverty guidelines and the minimum annual income required to be the sponsor of an immigrant:[15]

---

14 Sponsors on active duty with the US armed forces who are petitioning for their spouse or child are only required to demonstrate 100 percent of the poverty level.

15 These rates exclude Alaska and Hawaii.

Sponsor's Household Size	100% of HHS Poverty Guidelines	Immigration Sponsorship (125% of HHS)
2	$16,460	$20,575
3	$20,780	$25,975
4	$25,100	$31,375
5	$29,420	$36,775
6	$33,740	$42,175
7	$38,060	$47,575
8	$42,380	$52,975
	Add $4,320 for each additional person	Add $5,400 for each additional person

Table 2: 2018–19 HHS poverty guidelines

For example, Richard and Cecilia want to petition for their son to come to America from Peru. Their son is married with no children. Richard will be the petitioner and the financial sponsor. Richard must show that his income is at least 125 percent of the federal poverty level for a household of four people (Richard, his wife, his son, and his daughter-in-law). Therefore, he must have an annual income of at least $31,375 per year.

ASSISTING WITH FINANCIAL SPONSORSHIP

Not all petitioners earn enough money to serve as a sponsor. In this case, the US government is accommodating. The US government provides several options to allow people to qualify as sponsors. The following are some examples of how the US government helps if the sponsor's income is not enough:

Option One: Assets can be used towards the 125 percent of the federal poverty level. The sponsor can use the cash value of assets such as savings accounts, stocks, bonds, and property to complement their income to reach the minimum. For example, Richard can use the cash value of his savings account to increase his income.

Option Two: If assets are not enough, then members of the household can help. The income and assets of people related by birth, marriage, or adoption can be added. In our example, Richard can use the value of his wife's stocks and bonds to increase his income amount.

Option Three: The sponsor may count the assets of the foreign relatives. For instance, Richard can use the value of his son's house in Peru towards his income requirements.

Option Four: If all these options are not sufficient, the sponsor can use a joint sponsor. A joint sponsor is an additional person who is also willing to be the sponsor. The joint sponsor must meet all the same requirements as the main sponsor. However, the joint sponsor does not need to be related to the immigrant. Joint sponsors must reach the 125 percent income requirement on their own. They cannot combine their income with the assets of anyone else.

The petitioner has several opportunities to meet the

financial sponsorship requirements. More details on the options available for financial sponsors of immigrants may be found in the Consul's Corner.

BINDING THE SPONSOR

Financial sponsors must sign an affidavit of support (Form I-864). The affidavit of support is a legally enforceable document. It binds the US citizen or green card holder as the financial sponsor for an immigrant. Proof of income is required with the affidavit of support. This includes tax returns, bank account statements, and employment letters.

The sponsor's legal responsibility is not indefinite. It lasts until the immigrant becomes a US citizen, has ten years of work in the US, permanently leaves the US, or dies. The immigrant may sue the sponsor if they do not provide enough financial support.

The US government may also seek repayment for public benefits used by the immigrant. This includes food stamps, Medicaid, Temporary Assistance for Needy Families, Supplemental Security Income, or State Child Health Insurance benefits. It would be the sponsor who would need to pay the US government back for these services.

For years, this policy was not implemented. But, in May 2019, a memorandum from the White House addressed the issue and outlined a plan of action. It stated that government agencies must enforce all financial sponsorship regulations. This included suing the financial sponsors of immigrants who become a public charge.

Financial sponsorship is a requirement for any family-based immigrant visa application. The immigrant visa cannot be issued if the financial sponsorship is not in place. To see how the petitioning and sponsorship process works, let's look at my family as an example.

MY FAMILY'S MIGRATION STORY

Every immigrant has their own story about how they came to America. My family's story begins with my father, Sam. Sam came to the United States from Alexandria, Egypt, in the early 1970s. He came on a student visa to pursue his graduate studies. While living in America, he saw the opportunities and rewards for hard work that existed. He saw the United States as the beacon of opportunity and aspired to pursue the American dream for himself and his future family.

Upon completing his studies, he searched for a job to remain in America. A bank in Boston hired him and agreed to petition for him to receive an employment-based immigrant visa. For the visa to be issued, my father needed certification from the Department of Labor to prove he would not harm American workers by accepting this position.

Luckily, he received the certificate and his immigrant visa. Soon after his arrival in the US, his employer began the sponsorship process for my father to receive a green card.

My father later met my mother in Beirut, Lebanon. Back then, Beirut was in its heyday and known as the "Paris of the Middle East." Lebanon was (and still is) among the most beautiful holiday destinations, with both Mediterranean shores and snow-capped mountains. My father went to Lebanon for a visit with his family, who joined him there from Egypt. My mother was there on a university field trip from Alexandria.

They met in Beirut, and my father was enchanted with my mother. The fact that my mother was also from Alexandria, Egypt, sealed the deal for him to start wooing her. After my father returned to the US, and my mother to Egypt, the two exchanged written letters. My grandparents in Alexandria did their due diligence to approve of the union.

My parents then returned to Beirut to get married. The wedding was along the Mediterranean Sea, the place where they met less than a year earlier. At this point, my father was living and working in the United States as a green card holder. He wanted to bring his new bride home with him through the family-based immigrant visa process.

After getting married, my father began the petitioning process for his wife. The petition was for the spouse of a green card holder. My father served as the petitioner and financial sponsor for my mother. This immigrant visa category and type has a high number of visas allocated to it. My mother received her visa and joined my father in the US within months. They settled in South Boston and were keen to start a family.

I was born in Egypt and became an Egyptian citizen at birth. My father was the petitioner and financial sponsor for me to come to America. For her next pregnancy, my mother delivered in the United States. My brother received US nationality through birthright citizenship. Finally, my mother, father, and I were all naturalized as American citizens. We were a newly minted American family. The following is the letter we received from President Jimmy Carter when we became American citizens.

THE WHITE HOUSE
WASHINGTON

Dear Fellow American:

I congratulate you on becoming a citizen of our great nation.

Of very special importance is the fact that while many of us are citizens by birth, you have by choice selected America as your new land. The citizenship you have acquired today brings to you even greater guarantees of freedom, human dignity, security, equality and opportunity than those offered in the past. Your new citizenship gives you the right and also the responsibility to take part in the business of our government. I know you will hold strongly to these new rights and responsibilities and exercise them at every opportunity.

America has been blessed with almost boundless natural resources and wealth. Yet, its greatest asset continues to be its people. Our founding fathers had great faith in the worth of the individual. They believed that people from everywhere who loved freedom and justice should be entitled to enjoy these rich blessings. Thus they provided in the Constitution for the naturalization of such persons.

Naturalized citizens from all lands have made significant contributions to the betterment of our nation. I am sure that you will follow in this tradition and firmly resolve to do your part in making America an even more wonderful place in which to live.

Sincerely,

Jimmy Carter

Once my mother became an American citizen, she did what many new Americans do—begin the petition process to bring some of her family to America. Specifically, my mom embarked on the costly and time-consuming immigrant visa petitioning process for her younger brother, Michael.

My uncle Michael was known in Egypt as abu-shanab (father mustache) for his thick, lustrous mustache. He was a regular in the Alexandria expatriate scene. He was single and always ready to mingle with the Italians, Greeks, French, and Americans who lived in Alexandria. He dreamt of one day living in America, where he felt his personality would be more at home.

My mother could petition for her brother because he was the sibling of a US citizen. But my mother had trouble serving as the financial sponsor for my uncle. She had to show that she was making 125 percent of the federal poverty limit for a family of five people. This included herself, my father, my brother, my uncle, and me. Her income did not meet the requirements.

She thought about the options for petitioners who do not have the income to qualify as financial sponsors. The first option, using her other assets towards her income, did not work. She had a modest savings account, but the money in the account was not enough to reach the 125 percent threshold. With option two, though, my mother could use the income of her husband to complement her own. This worked—with my father's income, my mother was able to reach the 125 percent of the federal poverty limit requirement. She was able to sponsor her brother's immigrant visa application. My uncle Michael came to America and, eventually, also became an American citizen. We will meet more of my family who immigrated later.

THE GAP IN IMMIGRANT FINANCIAL SPONSORSHIP

It should be noted that the financial requirements to sponsor immigrants are not consistent with our immigration law. The law states that an immigrant cannot become a public charge, or depend on public assistance from American taxpayers. Yet the income requirements to sponsor an immigrant are less than the income requirements to qualify for public assistance. This is a contradiction of the law.

To make sense of this, let's look at the numbers. The income requirement to sponsor an immigrant is 125 percent of the federal poverty level. Based on the following table, a family of four, including the immigrant, must have a minimum income of $31,375.

Sponsor's Household Size	125% of Poverty Limit
2	$20,575
3	$25,975
4	$31,375
5	$36,775
6	$42,175
7	$47,575
8	$52,975
	Add $5,400 for each additional person

Table 3: 2018-19 HHS poverty guidelines

Now, compare this to the income requirements to qualify for public assistance. The Supplemental Nutrition Assistance Program (SNAP), formerly known as the Food Stamp Program, provides assistance for people in the United States buy food. A person may qualify for the SNAP if their household income is within 130 percent of the federal poverty level.

The following table provides the fiscal year 2018-19 SNAP annual income limits for eligibility.[16] Based on this table, a family of four would be required to have an income threshold of $32,640 to qualify for public assistance.

16   Does not include limits for Alaska and Hawaii.

Recipient's Household Size	130% of Poverty Limit
2	$21,408
3	$27,024
4	$32,640
5	$38,256
6	$43,872
7	$49,488
8	$55,104
	Add $5,616 for each additional person

Table 4: 2018–19 SNAP Annual Income Limits

A person who is making $31,400 to support four people can qualify to sponsor an immigrant—and also qualify for public assistance.[17] Our law is telling immigrants that they cannot have public assistance, but the sponsorship requirements are less than public assistance thresholds. This does not make sense.

The following table provides a side-by side comparison of the financial requirements to sponsor an immigrant and qualify for public assistance.[18] It shows how the financial requirements to sponsor an immigrant are less than the requirements to qualify for public assistance.

17 It is important to note that the Food and Nutrition Act of 2008 limits eligibility for SNAP benefits to US citizens and certain green card holders. To qualify for SNAP an immigrant must be under eighteen years old, have had their green card for five years, or be receiving disability-related assistance or benefits.

18 Does not include limits for Alaska and Hawaii.

Household Size	100% of HHS Poverty Guidelines	Immigrant Sponsor (125% of Poverty Limit)	SNAP Recipient (130% of Poverty Limit)
2	$16,460	$20,575	$21,408
3	$20,780	$25,975	$27,024
4	$25,100	$31,375	$32,640
5	$29,420	$36,775	$38,256
6	$33,740	$42,175	$43,872
7	$38,060	$47,575	$49,488
8	$42,380	$52,975	$55,104
	Add $4,320 for each additional person	Add $5,400 for each additional person	Add $5,616 for each additional person

Table 5: Annual income requirements to sponsor an immigrant compared to the annual income limit to qualify for SNAP

Simply put, the immigrant financial sponsorship requirement is inconsistent with immigration law. Our law tells immigrants that they cannot become a public charge, but it makes the financial requirement to sponsor an immigrant easier to qualify for than food stamps.

CLOSING THE GAP IN FAMILY-BASED IMMIGRATION SPONSORSHIP

It is important that immigration requirements reflect immigration law—that is, financial sponsorship requirements must reflect public charge laws. The minimum annual income requirements to sponsor an immigrant should be increased.

YOU BE THE CONSUL

Now it is time for you to be the consul. You are a consular officer at the US embassy in Costa Rica. A family-based immigration applicant arrives at your interview window. All their documents are in order. The medical report is fine. They have no disqualifying issues in their past.

The financial sponsorship documents show that the sponsor in the US has a family of three. The applicant has a child. The household will be five people. This means the sponsor will support a family of five.

The sponsor has an income of $36,900 per year. This qualifies him to be the financial sponsor for the applicants since the requirement is $36,775.

The problem is that this income also qualifies the family for public assistance. The requirement for SNAP is an income of no more than $38,256 for a family of five. The law states that immigrants cannot be a public charge. What would you do?

This is a dilemma. The law states one thing but the financial requirements to be a sponsor do not complement the law. You approve the immigration visa application. The sponsorship documents meet the financial requirements.

By issuing the immigrant visa you followed the law. But you also approved immigrants that could potentially become a public charge.

I recommend proposing a new rule to USCIS. While the current immigrant sponsorship requirement is 125 percent of the poverty level, the new rule would raise this to 150 percent based on the household size. This would ensure that the income to sponsor an immigrant is higher than the income limits to qualify for food stamps. It removes the ambiguity that currently exists, makes common sense, and enforces our immigration law.

IMPLEMENTATION

If the proposed rule is approved, the implementation of this recommendation is feasible. There is no new legislation required, as the recommendation helps to support the current public charge law. The financial sponsorship requirement would be the only thing changed—again, going from 125 percent of the federal poverty limit to 150 percent.

All government officials involved in deciding on the immigrant visa would use the new percentage—the rest of the sponsorship process would remain the same. This change is one that can be made in a timely manner.

The following table provides the annual income requirements to qualify for SNAP. This is compared to the immigrant sponsorship requirement at 150 percent of the federal poverty limit. Under the proposed adjustment, the amount to sponsor an immigrant would be more than the amount to qualify for public assistance.

Household Size	100% of HHS Poverty Guidelines	Immigrant Sponsor (150% of Poverty Limit)	SNAP Recipient (130% of Poverty Limit)
2	$16,460	$24,690	$21,408
3	$20,780	$31,170	$27,024
4	$25,100	$37,650	$32,640
5	$29,420	$44,130	$38,256
6	$33,740	$50,610	$43,872
7	$38,060	$57,090	$49,488
8	$42,380	$63,570	$55,104
	Add $4,320 for each additional person	Add $6,480 for each additional person	Add $5,616 for each additional person

A COMMON GROUND

To be clear, this recommendation is not intended to prevent low-income people from sponsoring immigrants, or to prevent low-income people from coming to America. The US government provides several options to help petitioners qualify as sponsors. If the petitioner still does not qualify, they can find a joint sponsor who will assist in the immigrant visa application process.

The purpose of this recommendation is to align immigration rules and laws—it is a common ground that all Americans can agree on.

CONCLUSION

The income requirements to sponsor an immigrant

should be more than the income to qualify for welfare. This is common sense and consistent with our law. The minimum annual income to sponsor an immigrant should be increased. I recommend that it is raised from 125 percent to 150 percent of the federal poverty level based on household size. Doing so would help us move towards a more pro-American immigration policy.

In this chapter, we reviewed a gap in the family-based immigration process—therefore, it only applies to relatives of American citizens and green card holders who want to come to America. In the following chapter, we will examine how the fiancés of American citizens would come to America. They are intending immigrants who are not yet related to American citizens and, within this grey area of visa processing, we will find yet another gap. We will review that gap and examine a reasonable solution for it.

THE CONSUL'S CORNER: FINANCIAL SPONSORSHIP REQUIREMENTS FOR FAMILY-BASED IMMIGRANT VISAS

A financial sponsor must meet certain income requirements to support an immigrant. You must show that your household income is equal to or higher than 125 percent of the US poverty level for your household size. Your household size includes the following:

- You

- Your dependents

- Any relatives living with you

- The immigrants you are sponsoring

If the sponsor is on active duty in the armed forces of the United States and the immigrant you are sponsoring is your spouse or child, your income only needs to equal 100 percent of the US poverty level for your household size.

If you cannot meet the minimum income requirements using your earned income, you have various options:

- You may add the cash value of your assets. This includes money in savings accounts, stocks, bonds, and property. To determine the amount of assets required to qualify, subtract your household income from the minimum income requirement (125 percent of the poverty level for your family size). You must prove the cash value of your assets is worth five times this difference (the amount left over).

  ◦ Exceptions:

    » If the person being sponsored is a spouse, or son/daughter (who is eighteen years or older) of a US citizen: The minimum cash value of assets must be three times the difference between the sponsor's household income and 125 percent of the federal poverty guideline for the household.

> » If the person being sponsored is an orphan coming to the United States for adoption: The adoptive parents' assets need to only equal or exceed the difference between the household income and 125 percent of the federal poverty line for the household size.

- You may count the income and assets of members of your household who are related to you by birth, marriage, or adoption.

  - ◦ To use their income you must have listed them as dependents on your most recent federal tax return or they must have lived with you for the last six months.

- You may count the assets of the relatives you are sponsoring.

*Data provided by the US Citizenship & Immigration Services

https://www.uscis.gov/greencard/affidavit-support

CHAPTER 6

---- ★ ----

FIANCÉ VISAS

INTRODUCTION

"Don't Mess with Cupid." It's not just an old Otis Redding song—it's an informal tenet of the US government. Americans fall in love with foreigners all the time. Accordingly, they may want to live as a married couple in the United States. For these couples, our government provides several options.

One of the options is the fiancé visa, also known as the K Visa. The fiancé visa is for partners of American citizens who want to come to the United States and get married within a short time. The fiancé visa is notorious within the United States. It gained notoriety from the San Bernardino terrorist attack in 2015—one of the murderers involved in the violence had immigrated to the US using a fiancé visa. The fiancé visa is what also inspired *90 Day Fiancé*, a hit American reality television series.

There is a critical hole in the fiancé visa application process—it allows a foreigner to come to America with the intention to immigrate, yet has none of the sponsorship requirements outlined in other visas. It doesn't make sense—why is it is easier for a fiancé to come to America than it is for the actual spouses of American citizens?

I recommend making the fiancé visa sponsorship process the same as the one for family-based immigrant visas. This would ensure that the sponsorship requirements for fiancés of American citizens who want to immigrate would be identical to those for the spouses of American citizens who want to do the same.

This recommendation ensures that a US citizen would take financial responsibility for the immigrant. It also ensures that there will be no complications when the fiancé eventually applies for their green card. This is important for American taxpayers—they are the ones who pay for the complications that arise when the immigrant is here.

I DO...BUT WHERE?

In the previous chapter, we discussed the migration story

of my family. We saw how my father immigrated to America, which led to my mother immigrating as well. My mother's immigration then led to her brother Michael's immigration to the US

My uncle Michael arrived in the US as a single guy. He began to establish himself as a carpenter and created a group of friends. He joined the local Coptic Orthodox Church in Jersey City. Most of his close acquaintances were other Egyptian immigrants.

He was pushing forty and started thinking about marriage. Michael's family back in Egypt encouraged him to "come home" to be introduced to some potential brides. This is a similar situation for many new immigrants. The concept of home becomes woven between the home that was left behind and the new home in America. Within this mindset, there is the idea that by marrying someone from the old home, the cultural, religious, and linguistic ties will then remain strong in the new home.

This is not unique to immigrant communities in America. We find the same phenomenon among the immigrants in the United Kingdom[19] and France.[20] Michael traveled to Egypt and, through some family introductions, met

19 Muttarak & Heath, "Who Intermarries in Britain?"

20 Safi & Godfrey, "Intermarriage and Assimilation."

Amal. After a brief courting period, and approval from the families, Michael and Amal got engaged.

Naturalized US citizens, such as Michael, are not the only Americans who get engaged to foreigners. Native-born Americans also fall in love and want to marry foreigners. There were 1.6 million married couples living in the US with one spouse who immigrated to the United States. So how do US citizens bring their partners to live in America? There are two primary options.

The first is to get married in the foreign fiancé's country. After marriage, the US citizen uses a family-based immigration visa petition to bring their new spouse to America. This is what my uncle did. Michael and his wife were both engaged and married in Egypt. After getting married, he petitioned and sponsored his new wife to come to America.

YOU BE THE CONSUL

Now it's time for you to be the consul. My uncle Michael had the option to marry his fiancé in the US using a fiancé visa. But my father did not have this option when marring my mother. Why was this?

If you say because my uncle was a US citizen at the time of his marriage while my father was a green card holder, then you are well on your way to becoming a consular officer.

The other way to marry a foreigner is to get engaged in a foreign country but married in the US. This requires the aforementioned fiancé visa—it is specifically for foreign fiancés of US citizens who want to get married in America. For more details on bringing a foreign spouse to the US, see the Consul's Corner on US immigration & marriage.

The fiancé visa permits the foreign fiancé to travel to the United States, but they must get married to their US citizen partner within ninety days of arrival. After the marriage, the foreign visa holder must apply for change of status. They change from a fiancé visa holder to a green card holder in the United States.

For example, if Michael and Amal wanted to get married in the US instead of Egypt, he would have then had to apply for a fiancé visa. Amal would have traveled to the US and they would have had to get married within the ninety-day period. Both options were available to them.

In the next section, we will examine the details of the fiancé visa to uncover the gap that exists in this immigration option.

FIANCÉ VISA: FROM TELEVISION TO TERRORISM

The history of the fiancé visa dates back to 1970s, when

the US was involved in the Vietnam War. During that time, Vietnamese citizens and US soldiers fell in love and wanted to get married. The Vietnamese citizen needed both an exit visa from the Vietnamese government and an immigrant visa from the US embassy. This was a time-consuming process—many couples could not complete the requirements before the US soldier returned back home.

At the same time, the Vietnamese citizen was not eligible for a tourist visa under INA 214(b). They wanted to marry an American citizen and, therefore, their intention was to immigrate to America. But, as you've learned, this reason would disqualify them from receiving a tourist visa. Many American-Vietnamese couples found themselves in a bind. Each member of the couple was in a different country and unable to be quickly united.

Vietnam veterans put pressure on Congress for a solution. In April 1970, Law 91-225 was passed. The new law amended the Immigration and Nationality Act and created the fiancé visa for partners of US citizens.

REQUIREMENTS

There are some requirements to qualify for the fiancé visa. The couple must have met in person at least once over a two-year period, although there are exceptions to this for extreme cultural or religious reasons. For example, the government makes an exception if there is a hardship for the US citizen to travel and personally meet the foreign fiancé. An exception can also be made if it is culturally inappropriate for a man and woman to meet before marriage.

The couple must also prove that they have a relationship. They can do this through pictures, testimonials, or engagement documents. The two people must be eligible to be married according to US laws—for example, they must both be of legal age and not already married to each other or to anyone else.

Since the fiancé visa leads to immigration, certain family-based immigration visa regulations also apply, such as rules that individuals who cannot pass a medical clearance or are addicted to drugs would not be eligible. Applicants who were previously deported from the US are also disqualified. The fiancé is also required to show that they will not be a public charge.

Fiancé visa applicants must attend an interview with a consular officer at a US consulate. There, the officer will question the applicant to ensure the relationship is legitimate and that all qualifications are met. If the officer gives the visa, the foreign fiancé may travel to the United States to live with the American fiancé. If the couple is not married within ninety days from the fiancé's arrival, the foreigner will no longer have legal status and must leave the country.

The television show *90 Day Fiancé* follows couples in the US that have fiancé visas. The program's storyline focuses on language barriers and culture shock—not to mention the stigma of being thought of as a mail-order bride. The international interactions with friends and family add to the intrigue.

The couple must overcome these obstacles and be married within the ninety-day period. Otherwise, as I have described, the fiancé visa expires and the foreign half of the couple must leave the United States. If they do not leave, they are then in the US illegally and face deportation. The television show was so popular that it inspired four spinoff series, which all focus on fiancé visa couples.

VULNERABLE TO FRAUD

The fiancé visa is not all lights, cameras, and action. The fiancé visa leads to immediate immigration and eligibility for employment in America, so it is an attractive option for people who want to come to the United States. As a result, it is considered to be a high fraud visa category and one that requires particular scrutiny. People can manufacture relationships, provide evidence of intent to marry in the US, and get their visas under false pretenses.

For example, in May 2019, US Immigration and Customs Enforcement (ICE) indicted over one hundred people. The group participated in a massive marriage fraud ring in Houston, Texas. They were creating fake engagements and marriages to help foreigners come to America.

Fiancé visas also have a high approval rate. This makes it tempting to try to use them to enter America. The Department of State has processed an average of 50,000 fiancé visas per year since 2013. From 2013 to 2015, the average refusal rate was 12 percent—which is low compared to other types of visas. For example, the average refusal rate for tourist visas during the same period was approximately 30 percent. For the period 2016-2018, the average refusal rate for fiancé visas rose slightly to 17 percent.

Year	Total Fiancé Visa Applications	Total Approved	Refusal Rate
2013	36,891	32,660	11%
2014	51,763	45,472	12%
2015	43,898	37,942	14%
2016	60,895	50,767	17%
2017	55,359	46,989	15%
2018	43,280	35,102	19%

Table 6: Fiancé Visa Adjudication Data

The refusal rate increased due to the terrorist attack in San Bernardino, California, during December of 2015. The attackers killed fourteen people, and injured twenty-two others, at a Christmas party—and one of the perpetrators had entered the US on a fiancé visa. After committing the mass shooting, they then tried bombing a building, the Inland Regional Center, in the town.

The deceased perpetrators, Syed Rizwan Farook and Tashfeen Malik, were a married couple. Farook was a US citizen, and his wife, Malik, was of Pakistani origin. Malik applied for a fiancé visa at the US embassy in Pakistan and, because of this, had undergone a security clearance process.

US government agencies had vetted her application and biometric information. They had compared her picture and fingerprints against national and international databases. The goal behind this process was to see if there were any matches with terror watch lists—and, for Malik, they found no red flags.

A consular officer in Pakistan approved Malik's fiancé visa. On July 27, 2014, she entered the United States, and the couple married. Less than eighteen months later, they committed the terrorist attack. This led to the increased scrutiny on fiancé visa applications.

THE GAP: FIANCÉS COME FOR FREE

Fiancé visas are in a grey area of visa processing at US consulates. The fiancé visa is classified as a nonimmigrant visa by the State Department. It is a nonimmigrant visa, like the ones issued to tourists, because the foreign fiancé does not have a legal family relationship to the petitioner. Since they are not married yet, the fiancé does not qualify for family-based immigration.

Although fiancé visas are considered nonimmigrant visas by the State Department, it is the immigrant visa sections at consulates that process them. This is because the fiancé is going to the US to get married and stay there—in practice, they are immigrating. The State Department's Worldwide NIV Workload by Visa Category Report documents this fuzzy situation. It states that fiancé visas "are more similar to an immigrant visa. As such, they are pre-processed in the immigrant operating system then moved to the non-immigrant operating system once a case has been deemed eligible for visa issuance."

NO PUBLIC CHARGE RESPONSIBILITY

This grey area in processing fiancé visa applications is what creates a gap and allows the visa to be exploited. Fiancé visas are like family-based immigrant visas—they need a medical clearance and are processed at immigrant visa sections at US consulates.

Yet, like nonimmigrant visas, fiancé visas do not require a financial affidavit of support. The requirement is that the applicant demonstrates that they can afford to go to America and get married. For this, the applicant can provide evidence of his or her own personal bank account. The American fiancé can also help—they can give their bank statements to show that they can afford to get married and support their spouse. This is what makes it similar to processing a tourist visa—the applicant must show that they can afford their visit to America, but they don't have to provide an affidavit of support.

The consular officer can make a decision on the fiancé visa application without an affidavit of support. This means that, if the visa is issued, there is no legal accountability. With no affidavit of support, no one is responsible in making sure the immigrant is not a public charge. There is no legal mechanism to enforce the public charge laws.

FINANCIAL REQUIREMENTS INCONSISTENT WITH THE LAW

Another problem comes if the consular officer does request an affidavit of support. The consular officer may request an affidavit of support from the applicant if they are apprehensive of the financial evidence provided.

In this case, the sponsor must submit an affidavit of support for fiancés. This form (I-134) is different than the form used for family-based immigrants (I-864). The main difference is the income requirements. The sponsor of a fiancé visa applicant only has to show an income of 100 percent of the federal poverty limit.

This creates several potential problems. The sponsorship requirements for fiancés are not in line with the law—the same issue we saw for family-based immigrants. The US law that states that immigrants cannot depend on public assistance also applies to foreign fiancés. But here, the problem is worst.

One hundred percent of the federal poverty level is far less than the threshold to qualify for food stamps. A person may qualify for SNAP if their household income is within 130 percent of the poverty level. Sponsors whose income is within 100 to 130 percent of the poverty level would qualify for food stamps.

Our law is telling immigrant fiancés that they cannot use public assistance. But the financial requirement to sponsor a fiancé is, once again, not consistent with the law.

The following table demonstrates the discrepancy. It shows the financial requirements to sponsor a fiancé if requested by the consular officer. It compares this against the income levels to qualify for public assistance. It is clear that the financial requirements to sponsor a fiancé are far less than the requirements to qualify for public assistance.

Household Size	Fiancé Visa Sponsor (100% of Poverty Limit)	SNAP Recipient (130% of Poverty Limit)
2	$16,460	$21,408
3	$20,780	$27,024
4	$25,100	$32,640
5	$29,420	$38,256
6	$33,740	$43,872
7	$38,060	$49,488
8	$42,380	$55,104

Table 7: Fiancé Visa Sponsorship vs. Public Charge

The immigrant financial sponsorship requirement is inconsistent with immigration law. It tells all sponsors and immigrants that the immigrant must be self-sufficient. It tells them they are not eligible for public assistance programs. At the same time, it allows people to sponsor fiancés with annual income levels that are so low that they could qualify for food stamps.

POTENTIAL DEPORTATION COSTS

There is a third problem for the US taxpayer. The fiancé visa allows the fiancé of a US citizen to travel to the United States and to marry within ninety days. Once the couple is married, the foreign spouse must immediately adjust their status. They go from a fiancé visa holder to a green card holder.

To do this, the American sponsor must complete a family-based immigrant visa petition. They must fulfill all the requirements for family-based immigration. The sponsor has to demonstrate that they are making 125 percent of the federal poverty limit. They must show that they are making 25 percent more when sponsoring the green card than when sponsoring the fiancé visa. That is a significant increase in income in only ninety days.

The following table illustrates the difference between the income to sponsor the fiancé before marriage and to apply for a green card after marriage. As you can see, the income needed to apply for the green card after marriage is higher than to sponsor the fiancé.

Household Size	Fiancé Visa Sponsor (100% of Poverty Limit)	Green Card Sponsor (125% of Poverty Limit)
2	$16,460	$20,575
3	$20,780	$25,975
4	$25,100	$31,375
5	$29,420	$36,775
6	$33,740	$42,175
7	$38,060	$47,575
8	$42,380	$52,975
	Add $4,320 for each additional person	Add $5,400 for each additional person

The American sponsor must show that they are making more money. If not, they will need to find a joint sponsor. If they cannot do this, then the foreign spouse will not qualify for a green card. This means that the foreign spouse will be living in the US illegally and need to be deported. These cases are rare, but, when they happen, there is a cost to taxpayers. Deportation proceedings require lawyers, judges, law enforcement, and other costs. These are all paid for with public funds.

The process to carry out deportation is already costing taxpayers millions. According to the US Immigration and Customs Enforcement, there were, on average, 72,000 deportations per year from 2015-2017. Each deportation costs the American taxpayer approximately $10,800. That is more than three quarters of a billion dollars spent on deportation in three years. It is in the interest of the American people to find ways to reduce the number of people that may need to be deported.

ICE Deportations

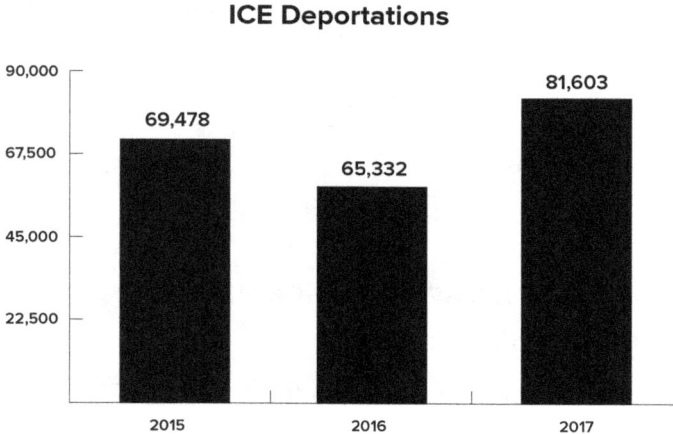

Figure 2: ICE Deportations 2015-2017

Let's go back to the fiancé visa applicant that you interviewed. The US sponsor was making $17,000 when you issued the visa. This amount qualified the fiancé to get the fiancé visa, travel to the US, and get married.

Within three months of arriving in the US, the couple got married. The foreign spouse applies for a green card. Now the sponsor has to show that he is making at least $20,575 per year for a family of two. This means that the American spouse needs an extra $3,575 in income.

The American sponsor does not have this money. He also cannot find a joint sponsor who will take financial responsibility for his wife. The foreign spouse will not qualify for a green card. This means she will be living in the US illegally and need to be deported.

Your decision to issue a visa to this applicant was justified. You followed the requirements for financial sponsorship for fiancés. But your decision also caused a problem for the American taxpayer. As a consular officer, you should not be faulted. The requirements for fiancé visas need to change to be in line with family-based immigrant visas.

CLOSING THE GAP IN FIANCÉ VISA SPONSORSHIP

Fiancé visa applicants are intending to marry a US citizen and live in America. Fiancés are intending immigrants, and they should be processed as immigrants. They should fall under the same requirements as family-based immigrant visas.

Most of the process is already aligned between fiancé visas and family-based immigrant visas. Both require a petition application, police certification, medical clearance, and security clearance. The only major difference in the documentation is the affidavit for financial sponsorship.

I recommend proposing a regulation to the Department of State. The new rule would require fiancés to be treated like spouses. Fiancés must submit the same financial sponsorship affidavit as family-based immigrants. The fiancé's sponsor must also show the same income as a spouse's sponsor. In other words, a fiancé should follow the same guidelines as a spouse.

This new rule supports the enforcement of the current law INA 212 (a)(4). This recommendation makes sense for US immigration policy as it kills several birds with one stone.

First, there will be a financial sponsorship requirement for sponsoring fiancés. A US citizen will be legally and financially responsible for the foreign fiancé.

Second, we will reduce the risk of fiancé visa applicants becoming a public charge. They will follow the same financial guidelines as family-based immigrants. In chapter 5, I recommended increasing the income requirements to sponsor an immigrant. It would become 150 percent of the federal poverty level. The fiancé will have to follow the same rule. This is in line with US immigration law that immigrants not be a public charge.

Third, there will be no complications later in the adjustment of status process. The financial requirements to apply for a green card will be done at the US consulate while applying for the visa. It will be taken care of before the fiancé arrives in America. This will reduce the chances of potentially deporting the foreign spouse. It also avoids having additional immigrants in the US that are out of status. This prevents unnecessary costs to the US taxpayer.

Some lawmakers are reluctant to make changes to the fiancé visa process. They do not want to undermine a program that supports marriage. After the San Bernardino shooting, Representative Steve King (R-Iowa) said that Congress is hesitant to put restrictions on fiancé visas. "[Congress doesn't] want to cross Cupid...why would you interrupt a visa that's designed to put people together and start new families?"[21] The recommendation made here can be implemented without disturbing these lawmakers (or Cupid).

---

21   Min Kim, "Finance visas off limits in rush to tighten borers."

Implementing this recommendation is feasible—it does not need any new documentation. Fiancés would use the same affidavit of support as family-based immigrants (I-864). The US government has used this form for decades. There would not be any special restrictions placed on fiancés—they would simply follow the same sponsorship rules as spouses of US citizens. This should quell the concerns of members of Congress who don't want to cross Cupid.

The recommendation would also not need any new laws. Immigrant public charge laws already exist. Using an affidavit of support for immigrants has been in place for over twenty years. State Department officials are already familiar with the law and documentation.

Finally, the State Department procedure to process fiancé visas would remain the same. Fiancé visa applications are already being preprocessed in the State Department's immigrant visa operating system. Also, immigrant visa sections of US consulates are already processing fiancé visas. This would continue to be the case—there would be no disturbance to the operations at consulates.

The only difference is that fiancés will be treated like spouses who want to come to America. The fiancé's sponsor will need to provide the same affidavit of support as a spouse's sponsor. They will also need to demonstrate the same amount of income.

A COMMON GROUND

Americans want reasonable immigration policy that protects the interests of the United States. Americans would agree that treating fiancés like spouses in the immigration process is reasonable. After all, a fiancé is just another name for a future spouse.

This recommendation does not limit fiancés from coming to America. It does not prevent them from marrying their American partners. Instead, it protects the foreign fiancé and American partner. They will be able to avoid complications in the green card process down the line. It also protects American citizens—they will not have to pay for the costs of legal action and even deportation procedures. All potential hurdles are handled before the fiancé arrives in America.

This recommendation encourages sponsorship requirements for fiancés that are in line with our immigration law. It removes a weakness in immigration policy that can be manipulated to the disadvantage of the American taxpayer.

CONCLUSION

Under our current laws, it is easier to bring a foreign fiancé to America that it is to bring a foreign spouse. You have a legally binding relationship with a spouse, but the immigration process is easier for a fiancé. This is not consistent with the law—it is not even consistent with common sense.

We need a rule that is more logical. We need a rule that makes the requirements for fiancés to come to America at least the same as spouses. This makes the financial sponsorship for fiancés consistent with immigration law. It helps us move towards a more pro-American immigration policy.

In the next chapter, we shift our attention to immigrants who come to America because of a stroke of luck. They do not have family in America or an employer that is sponsoring them. Instead, they are winners of the diversity visa lottery program. Winning this lottery is a dream for many foreigners, but not all Americans are supportive of the program. We will look at how to make this lottery program more beneficial to Americans. I will recommend meritizing the diversity visa program.

THE CONSUL'S CORNER: US IMMIGRATION & MARRIAGE

A US citizen has several ways to bring a foreign fiancé or spouse (husband or wife) to the United States to live:

- Visa for fiancé of a US citizen:

  - K: Requires a foreigner to marry his or her US citizen fiancé within ninety days of entry or depart the United States. Once the couple marries, the foreign citizen must adjust status to become a lawful permanent resident of the United States (green card holder).

- Immigrant visa for a spouse of a US citizen:

  - IR1: The Immediate Relative 1(IR1) visa IR1 is for couples married for longer than two years.

  - CR1: The Conditional Resident 1 (CR1) visa is for couples married less than two years.

- Nonimmigrant visa for spouse of a US citizen:

  - K-3: This visa category is intended to shorten the physical separation between the foreign citizen and US citizen spouses by having the option to obtain a nonimmigrant K-3 visa overseas and enter the United States to await approval of the immigrant visa petition.

A US green card holder has only one way to bring a foreign spouse (husband or wife) to the United States to live:

- Immigrant visa for spouse and minor children of green card holders:

  - F2A: Family Preference category 2(FP2)

*Data provided by the US Department of State Bureau of Consular Affairs (www.travel.state.gov).

CHAPTER 7

---- ★ ----

DIVERSITY VISA

INTRODUCTION

Imagine winning the lottery. After buying your lottery ticket, you turn on the television and watch for the winning numbers. One by one, the balls pop up to the surface in the lottery-drawing machine. The first five numbers are correct, and you have one more to go.

You take a quick peek at your lottery ticket to make sure you know the number you need—it's an eight. By this time, you are within inches of the television with your fingers and toes crossed. You yell, "Come on, lucky number eight!" The ball pops up and it's an eight! You don't believe it. You take another look at the ticket and then again at the television. It sets in—you just won millions of dollars!

You throw your arms in the air and jump for joy. This is going to change your life. You can get the house that you couldn't afford, pay off your kid's student loans, and even donate to your favorite charity. You are now a lucky lottery winner.

Every year 50,000 people around the world win a lottery. But their prize is not cash—it's a US green card. The diversity immigrant visa (DV) program gives people the chance to win immigration to America. In 2018, 14.7 million people registered for the program. They had a better chance of winning a green card than winning the New York lottery.

To win a diversity visa, you don't need family members to petition for you. You don't need a financial sponsor or employment. You don't even need to wait for years for your application to be processed. All you need is the desire to immigrate to the US and some luck. While winning the DV is a dream for some, it is a nightmare for others. Some Americans believe the diversity visa lottery program brings over more people who will compete for American jobs.

There is a gap in the diversity visa lottery program. It does not factor in how immigrant visa winners can complement American economy and society. There must be a way to ensure that Americans benefit from these 50,000 new immigrants each year.

In this chapter, I recommend meritizing the DV program. This means making academic, professional, and personal skills part of the selection criteria. This will create a mutually beneficial relationship between America and the diversity visa winners. The diversity visa is an excellent tool in US foreign policy—it keeps the American dream alive around the world. Then again, pursing diversity should not be at the detriment of the American people.

REQUIREMENTS FOR A DIVERSITY VISA

The diversity visa program was established as part of the Immigration Act of 1990, which was signed into law by President George H. W. Bush. It established that 55,000 immigrant visas would be available annually to diversify the countries where immigrants come from. People born in countries with low rates of immigration to the US could apply for the diversity visa.

The government defines a low rate of immigration as a country that sent less than 50,000 immigrants to the US in the previous five years. Some countries with low rates of immigration to the US include Thailand, Kuwait, Ethiopia, Finland, and New Zealand. In 1999, the number of available diversity visas was reduced from 55,000 to 50,000.

Diversity visa applicants are not required to have a US

citizen petitioner or sponsor. This is different than other immigrant visas. In fact, the application process for the diversity visa process is quite simple. Online applications are accepted during a one-month period in the fall of each year. It is free to apply, and each qualifying family member can submit an application. This maximizes the chances of the family winning.

To qualify as a diversity visa applicant, the person must have a high school diploma or two years of work experience. The work experience must be in the last five years in an occupation that the US Department of Labor defines. These requirements only apply to the primary applicant. Dependents, such as a spouse or unmarried children under twenty-one, do not need to fill the requirements. For more details on requirements, please see the Consul's Corner on diversity visa eligibility.

Winning application numbers are selected using a randomized computer drawing system. The Department of State randomly selects about 120,000 applicants. The first 50,000 people selected are the finalists, and the rest are on a waiting list. More than 50,000 people are selected because it is likely that some of the finalists will not qualify for visas.

When I adjudicated diversity visa applications, I disqualified many finalists. Some did not appear for the interview, or they came without all of the required documentation. Diversity visa applicants are required to meet medical and security clearances. Many are disqualified for having a type of disease or criminal record that precludes them from immigrating to the US.

As finalists are disqualified, applicants on the waiting list are called for an interview. The first 50,000 to have their diversity visa issued are the official winners of that year's visa lottery. The diversity visa winner can immigrate to the US with their spouse and any unmarried children under twenty-one years of age.

THE CONTROVERSY OF DIVERSITY

Three years ago, I was looking for an apartment in Hoboken, New Jersey. On a sunny, Thursday afternoon, my agent took me to see a two-bedroom in a traditional brownstone. The owner's agent, Carlo, was waiting for us at the building. He was a tall, impeccably dressed guy in his early thirties. We walked up the stairs, and he showed us around the apartment. He described the damaged wood flooring as "part of the charm." I could not help but notice his accent while he spoke—it was unmistakably English with a strong Italian slant. I'm pretty sure my agent was more interested in Carlo than making the sale.

As we walked downstairs, I asked where he was from and,

unsurprisingly, he said a town in the south of Italy. He immigrated to the US only three years before and had become one of the top real estate agents in town. My consular training makes it impossible for me to hear about immigration and not ask questions. I asked if he came to the US to join family or if his employer sponsored his immigrant visa. To my shock, he told me that he came to the US after winning the green card lottery.

This surprised me. I had adjudicated hundreds of diversity visa applications—but I had never randomly met someone in the US who had won one. Before coming to America, Carlo worked in retail in Italy. He applied for the diversity visa because one of his colleagues told him about it. He never thought he would win. He was wrong—he won the diversity visa the first time he applied for it.

He came to America to pursue his dream of becoming a real estate developer. Judging by the short time he took to establish himself in the real estate space, he is well on his way. I did not end up taking the apartment from Carlo, but I did get to meet a diversity visa winner on the other side of the interview window.

Carlo is very grateful for the diversity visa program. Yet, in the US, the program has been controversial for decades. Many Americans don't see the point of allowing people to immigrate to the US only to increase the diversity of immigrants. Others feel that the 50,000 diversity visas for people who have no ties to the US can be better used for family members. Another major concern is that it allows potential terrorists to enter our country.

SECURITY CONCERNS

Not all diversity visa recipients are like Carlo. Abdurasul Juraboev and Sayfullo Saipov were diversity visa winners. Juraboev was from Uzbekistan. He plead guilty to conspiring to provide material support to the Islamic State. On October 27, 2017, he was sentenced to fifteen years in prison.

Days later, Saipov, also from Uzbekistan, plowed a truck into a bike lane along the Hudson River in lower Manhattan. The rampage ended when he crashed into a school bus and was shot by the police. After being arrested, he admitted that he supported the Islamic State. He used a truck as a weapon in order to inflict maximum damage against civilians.

Hesham Hadayet, an Egyptian born immigrant to the US, benefited from his wife winning the diversity visa. His wife was the primary applicant, and he immigrated to the US as the spouse. On July 4, 2002, Hadayet walked into Los Angeles Airport and opened gunfire. He killed two people and was shot and killed by the police. These acts of terrorism have led people to associate the diversity visa program with terrorists. In fact, Steven Camarota called the diversity visa program "ideally suited for terrorists."[22]

The reality, however, is that the DV is not prone to terrorists. DV applicants go through the same security background clearance as all other immigrants. The consular officer collects biometric data during the interview, which includes fingerprints and pictures. The data is then analyzed for multiple confirmations of identity.

All applicants over sixteen years old must go through the same process. It starts with providing a police report from their country of residence. The applicant also provides a police report from all countries lived in for a year or more. For example, Inma is an eighteen-year-old woman from Spain. She studied in Paris for a year. Therefore, she has to provide a police report from both Spain and France.

Applicants must also provide certified copies of each court and prison record, if they were convicted of any crimes. For example, an applicant is a resident of South Africa and lived in Belgium for only eight months. While in Belgium, he was convicted for driving while intoxicated. He must provide a police certificate from South Africa. He must also provide certified copies of the police reports from Belgium.

22   Camarota, "Trump's Right. End the diversity visa lottery."

The consular officer may also request a security advisory opinion (SAO). The SAO is also called a security clearance, administrative clearance, or administrative processing. Consular officers all over the world use the SAO process—it confirms that the applicant is not known by the US government to have criminal ties. This is critical in deciding to approve a case or not.

The process starts with the consular officer. He or she sends a request from the consulate to the Department of State's headquarters. The request is to investigate the visa applicant for possible illegal activity. This includes espionage, terrorism, criminal activity, financial crimes, and illegal export of technology.

The Department of State will do the initial check. Then it works with other agencies to do a comprehensive background check. The process involves the Department of Homeland Security, the Federal Bureau of Investigation (FBI), the Central Intelligence Agency (CIA), the Drug Enforcement Administration (DEA), the Department of Commerce, the Department of the Treasury's Office of Foreign Assets Control, and, at times, the International Police (Interpol).

The SAO process takes time. Some visa applicants are cleared in a matter of weeks, and some have undergone administrative processing for much longer. There were cases in which I requested an SAO from Washington, DC, and I did not receive the clearance for over a year. I saw visa applicants lose jobs at hospitals and technology companies. Their employers could not afford to keep the position open while the applicant waited for the SAO clearance to arrive.

I was sympathetic with the frustration of applicants who lost positions in America; still, I could not approve a visa before the SAO clearance was received from Washington, DC. The US government has tried to make the SAO process more efficient. In 2016, the Department of State called for a complete review of the SAO process. That same year, it also implemented new technical and business processes in data sharing. This was to help hurry the communication across agencies and speed up decisions on SAOs.

Regardless of the desire to improve the SAO process, the reality is that security comes first. The required time will always be taken for all agencies to do their due diligence. Nobody in the US government wants to be responsible for letting a terrorist into the United States—I can assure you of this.

ATTEMPTS TO TERMINATE DIVERSITY VISAS

Concerns over the diversity visa lottery led to several

attempts to end the program. In December 2005, the House of Representatives voted to add an amendment to the border enforcement bill to abolish the program. But the Senate never passed the bill. In March 2007, Congressman Bob Goodlatte (R-VA) introduced the Security and Fairness Enhancement for America Act. It sought to eliminate the visa lottery program, yet the diversity visa survived.

In May 2009, Representative Goodlatte reintroduced his Security and Fairness Enhancement for America Act. The bill would have amended the Immigration and Nationality Act to end the diversity visa program. This bill did not pass. In 2013, the "Gang of Eight" drafted the Border Security, Economic Opportunity, and Immigration Modernization Act. The bill would have repealed the diversity visa program. The bill died in the House of Representatives and, once again, the program survived.

The diversity visa program came into existence three decades ago. Since then, there have been at least five attempts to end it. This tells us that there are serious concerns about the diversity visa program. Still, none of the attempts to end the diversity visa program have succeeded. This also tells us something.

The solution to do away with the diversity visa program may not be the right answer. There is a reason these attempts failed—most Americans believe that people deserve the possibility to pursue prosperity. The reality is that, for most people all over the world, the United States is the best place to do this. This is to our advantage as a country.

Most people will never be able to come to America, but the diversity visa offers the possibility. This possibility is important for the United States to maintain its "soft power" in the world. Soft power is an approach in international diplomacy—it involves the use of economic, political, and cultural influence in interactions with other countries.

The US government partners with athletes, artists, and even TV producers to engage with people in other countries. They meet with local counterparts to exchange ideas and expertise. For example, Andre and Maria Jacquemetton, award-winning writers and producers, led workshops on scriptwriting and storytelling for media students in Bahrain. The US embassy organized this event where the Bahraini students got to hang out with the producers of the American hit television show *Mad Men*.

This is only one example of how the United States pursues soft power. This is the opposite of hard power, which involves military might to influence decisions. The two types of power complement each other. Military leaders will often say that the use of soft power helps avoid the use of hard power. The diversity visa program, and the chance for foreigners to pursue the American dream, contributes to America's soft power in the world.

This is not to say that all Americans are in love with the diversity visa program. In January 2009, Representative Sheila Jackson-Lee (D-TX) introduced the Save America Comprehensive Immigration Act. The bill would have doubled the number of diversity visas available to 110,000 yearly. This bill did not pass either.

Therefore, the answer is not to expand or to end the diversity program. Instead, it makes sense to figure out a way to make the program more in line with the needs of the American people. To do this, let's identify the gap in the diversity visa program.

THE GAP: IGNORING AMERICA'S ECONOMIC NEEDS

The diversity visa program does not take into consideration the needs of the US economy in the selection process. The diversity visa program only focuses on geographic diversity. The Consul's Corner on diversity visa eligibility shows that, to receive the diversity visa, the applicant must be born in specific countries. They only need a high school education or two years of experience in the last five years.

YOU BE THE CONSUL

Now it's time for you to be the consul. You are at the US embassy in Paris. At your interview window is Felipe, a lucky diversity visa finalist. He completed his high school studies five years ago. But he decided not to go to college because higher education is not for him. Instead, he spends most of his time at local coffee shops. He talks about sports and politics with other buddies from the neighborhood.

He is not working. He is not worried about finding a job because he receives some of his father's pension funds. He also has some savings thanks to his parents. He comes to his immigrant visa interview, and you are the interviewing officer. He provides all the required documents such as his high school diploma. His security clearance is clean.

Would you issue Felipe a visa? Since Felipe meets all qualifications, the answer is yes. He is now a lucky diversity visa winner.

Thomas is also a diversity lottery finalist. He did not finish high school because his father became ill and he needed to support his family. He had to drop out during his senior year. But for the past four years he has worked as a long haul tractor-trailer truck driver. Over the years he learned how to maintain trucks. He can check vehicles to ensure that the mechanical, safety, and emergency equipment are in good shape. He maintains logs of vehicle service and repair status to be in line with local regulations. His supervisor gave him a raving letter of support for the visa interview. He is excited to attend his interview. He knows that he has good work experience and that truck drivers are in demand in the United States.

Would you give Thomas a visa? In this case the answer is no. You would not issue the visa because he does not have a high school diploma. Also, his experience as a truck driver does not qualify him for the visa.

This means that people who have not been productive in three out of the past five years can qualify for the diversity visa. It also means that anyone with a high school diploma can qualify. People who qualify under these rules may not be of particular benefit to the US economy. The criteria in awarding the diversity visa does not specify the specialized skills required by the US. In other words, there is no mechanism to ensure the potential diversity visa immigrant will be of benefit to the American people.

The American people would probably not benefit from Felipe. If he is unproductive in his country, there is little evidence that he will be of benefit to the United States. Still, he met the qualifications and received a visa. On the other hand, the American people may have benefited from Thomas. With his truck driving skills, Thomas could fill a demand in the current US job market. Truck drivers were among the ten most in-demand jobs in the United States in 2018.[23] Thomas' work ethic and motivation show that he would likely be productive in America, but he did not meet the qualifications.

The gap is that the diversity visa program does not take into account the benefits that the winner may provide to the US economy. The diversity visa cannot be to the detriment of American productivity—we need a way

---

23   Long, "America has a massive truck driver shortage."

of ensuring that the US profits from these 50,000 new immigrants each year.

CLOSING THE GAP: A MERIT-BASED DIVERSITY VISA

I recommend proposing a regulation to the Department of State that instead selects diversity visa winners based on merit. Their "luck" will depend on how much they can contribute to the American economy and society. Qualification will no longer only be based on location or if they have a high school diploma.

A merit-based immigration system is one based on points. This is different than family-based immigration that depends on family ties or employment-based immigration that depends on professional ties. Under a meritized diversity visa program, an applicant's eligibility is based on points they earn. Applicants earn points based on different criteria, such as language fluency, education level, age, professional skills, and extraordinary achievements.

The number of points allocated to each criterion is based on the priorities of the United States. For example, if the United States wants diversity immigrants in their twenties, the number of points awarded to someone who is twenty-five would be ten. On the other hand, someone who is forty-five would only receive four points.

If the United States wants people who speak English, a higher number of points would be awarded to applicants with high scores on a standardized English exam such as the TOEFL. If the United States wants truck drivers, nurses, or software developers more points would be awarded to applicants with these professional skills.[24]

Making the diversity visa merit-based is important. It will help address the specialized skills required by the United States. This is not to say that only highly skilled professionals would qualify for the diversity visa. In the United States, there's a need for different types of skills—there is a need for engineers in Silicon Valley and truck drivers in the transportation industry. What skills are valued will depend on the needs of the US economy.

IMPLEMENTATION

Implementation of this recommendation would need coordination across government agencies. The US Department of Labor publishes an Employment Projections Report, which places estimates of what the American labor market will need ten years into the future. For example, for 2016–2026, the healthcare and social assistance sector will be the fastest growing industry. The report also found that manufacturing would decrease in the coming years.

---

24   These are three of the top ten needed jobs in the US as of 2018.

The Department of Labor publishes the Occupational Outlook Handbook as well. It provides details on percentage changes in occupations over the next ten years. For example, personal care aids will be the fastest-growing job by 2026.

The Department of State and Department of Labor could create a diversity visa joint committee. The committee would determine the labor priorities for the diversity visa on a five-year basis. They could use the reports that are already published by the Department of Labor to determine the priorities.

For example, they may decide that we need personal care aids in their thirties. We may need female software engineers or heavy-tractor-trailer truck drivers that speak English. Based on these priorities, the committee allocates points to the criteria on the application.

The diversity visa online application will need to be expanded. It should include more detailed questions about the applicant's personal and professional background. The applicant would gain points based on how they answer the questions. The higher the applicant ranks, the better their chances are to be a diversity visa lottery finalist.

The selection of the application number would still be

random, but the pool of applicants to select from would not be. It would include applicants that are consistent with the needs set by the US government. The new process accounts for the diverse skill requirements of the United States. People who win diversity visas will have profiles that are in line with our country's economic needs.

A COMMON GROUND

Meritizing the diversity visa program is a reasonable, common ground action—it is something most Americans can agree on. First, it introduces merit into the US immigration process. Merit does not have a role in today's immigration process, and Americans have expressed an interest in changing this. President Trump made a plea for merit-based migration in the 2018 State of the Union Address. "It is time to begin moving towards a merit-based immigration system—one that admits people who are skilled, who want to work, who will contribute to our society, and who will love and respect our country," he said.

The Trump administration is not the first to propose a merit-based immigration system. President George W. Bush preferred a merit-based system—he included it as part of his 2007 immigration reform bill. However, that proposal did not pass in the Senate.

Second, this recommendation incorporates merit without

changing the entire immigration system. Diversity visas account for less than 10 percent of annual immigrants to America. Family-based immigration and employment-based immigration will continue as normal.

This is a compromise for Americans who do not want an immigration system that is only merit-based. For example, in May 2019, Trump announced a plan to restructure US immigration. He sought to transform it into a merit-based immigration system. His opponents did not agree. For example, Senator Richard Blumenthal (D-Conn) declared the merit-based immigration plan as "dead on arrival." Meritizing only the diversity visa is a reasonable compromise.

Third, this recommendation keeps the door open to foreigners who dream of coming to America. The element of chance will continue to exist—people who do not have family ties or job offers in America may still be able to come if their backgrounds can benefit our country.

Finally, the program will continue to diversify the profile of immigrants to America. This was the original vision of the program. Instead, however, the diverse profiles will address the needs of our economy.

Today, the requirements to qualify for the diversity visa are insufficient. One only needs a high school diploma and to be born in a country with low rates of immigration. This is to the advantage of foreigners, not Americans. We need to have diversity visa winners who complement America's needs, as this will be to everyone's advantage.

CONCLUSION

Each year, 50,000 new immigrants and their families come to the US using the diversity visa lottery program. These new immigrants diversify where people come from, but this is not enough. There needs to be a clear benefit of the diversity visa program to the American people and society.

Meritizing the diversity visa program helps achieve this. The more applicants' profiles match the needs of US society, the better chance they should have to become diversity visa winners. This creates a beneficial relationship for the diversity visa winner and the American people. It helps us move towards a more pro-American immigration policy.

In the next chapter, we will examine our final gap in immigration policy. We move away from immigrant visas and focus on green cards. Green cards are officially called "lawful permanent residency cards." They are given to immigrants who should be permanently living in the United States. Yet our policy allows green card holders to not live in the United States and still maintain all their rights as green card holders. I will encourage you to demand putting the "permanent" back into lawful permanent resident.

THE CONSUL'S CORNER: DIVERSITY VISA ELIGIBILITY REQUIREMENTS

There are only two requirements to be eligible to apply for the diversity visa:

- Requirement one: Individuals born in countries whose natives qualify may be eligible to enter.

  - If you were not born in an eligible country, there are two other ways you might be able to qualify.

    » Was your spouse born in a country whose natives are eligible? If yes, you can claim your spouse's country of birth—provided that both you and your spouse are named on the selected entry, are found eligible and issued diversity visas, and enter the United States simultaneously.

    » Were you born in a country whose natives are ineligible but in which neither of your parents was born or legally resident at the time of your birth? If yes, you may claim the country of birth of one of your parents if it is a country whose natives are eligible for the program.

- Requirement two: Each diversity visa applicant must meet the education/work experience requirement of the diversity visa program by having either of the following:

  - At least a high school education or its equivalent, defined as successful completion of a twelve-year course of formal elementary and secondary education

  - Two years of work experience within the past five years in an occupation that requires at least two years of training or experience to perform. The

Department of State will use the US Department of Labor's O*Net Online database to determine qualifying work experience.

*Data provided by the US Department of State Bureau of Consular Affairs

https://travel.state.gov/content/travel/en/us-visas/immigrate/diversity-visa-program-entry.html

CHAPTER 8

———— ⋆ ————

GREEN CARD

INTRODUCTION

She took out a pair of scissors. Piece by piece, my grand-mother Aida shredded her green card until it was no more. "Now I don't have a choice," she said. Many people would say it was crazy of Aida to tear up her green card. People do all sorts of things to try and get an American green card, and here Aida was destroying it.

The concept of a green card entered popular culture thanks to the 1990 film entitled *Green Card*. The film was a popular romantic comedy directed by Peter Weir. It starred Gérard Depardieu and Andie MacDowell. The movie was about an American woman who married a French man just so that he could get a green card and stay in America.

In real life, this type of arrangement is called a marriage of convenience. Usually the foreigner pays money for the service. This is illegal, and the American can face criminal charges if the marriage is proven to be fake.

Millions of people spend a lot of time, money, and energy to get a green card, and Aida just gave it up. She destroyed her green card, but not because she had any ill feeling towards the United States. She just didn't want to have to live in America to maintain her status.

In theory, she was right. Having a green card means that a person is a lawful permanent resident (LPR) in America. As the name says, the person should be lawfully and permanently residing in the United States until they become a citizen.

In practice, the situation is different. People from all over the world, ones who are not living in America, still have American green cards. They can even exercise important rights. One of the most important of these rights is to petition for other family members to immigrate to the US. For example, my grandmother was not a US citizen, nor was she permanently living in the US. But, with her green card, she could petition for her daughter to immigrate to America. Why do our policies allow non-US citizens who are not living in the US to petition for others to come to America?

In this chapter, we will review the requirements to maintain a green card. We will also learn about the privileges that come with it. As I have mentioned, we will see that there are lawful permanent residents of the US that are not permanently living in America. In spite of this, they enjoy the full rights and privileges offered to green card holders.

I will recommend that a physical presence requirement be placed on green card holders that want to bring family members to come to America. They would have to live in the US for at least twelve consecutive months just before being able to petition for others. This ensures that green card holders can exercise their most important right only when actually living in America. It's time to put the "permanent" back into "lawful permanent resident."

PERMANENT RESIDENTS AREN'T ALWAYS PERMANENT

A lawful permanent resident card, or green card, is given to a foreigner who has immigrated to America but is not yet a citizen. So far, we've discussed how people immigrate to America. We saw family-based immigration, such as my mother and my uncle. We discussed employment-based immigration, such as my father. We also examined diversity-based immigration, such as Carlo, the real estate agent in New Jersey.

In all these cases, the foreigners receive an immigrant visa at a US consulate to move to the United States. After arriving in America, the new immigrant applies for their green card. This card identifies the person as a legal resident.

To maintain a green card, the immigrant cannot be outside the US for more than a year at a time. They must also not have the intention to permanently move to another country. For example, Joanne immigrated to America from Argentina. She received her green card, and afterward, she went back to Argentina for eight months. But her intentions are not to permanently stay in Argentina. Joanne's green card will continue to be valid when she returns to America after the eight months. The Consul's Corner on lawful permanent residency status provides more details.

The green card comes with many rights and privileges. It allows the immigrant to legally live and work in America. Green card holders can receive American scholarships and in-state tuition benefits. They are protected by US jurisdiction and can even travel to some countries without a visa. But there are two particularly important rights— green card holders can become naturalized US citizens, and they can also apply for other foreign family members to immigrate to America.

You would think that to exercise all these rights, the immigrant should be living in America. A few years ago, I was talking with an immigration lawyer. He told me, "Isn't it ironic that the green card is called a lawful permanent residency card? It's not really permanent—it expires every ten years." I was flabbergasted.

The "permanent" in a lawful permanent residency card is not referring to the expiration date. It is referring to the fact that the green card holder should be permanently living in America. What is ironic is that so many people have lawful permanent residency cards but do not live in America. Even more ironic is that this has become commonplace. Some immigration professionals have become blind to the concept of "permanent" in the legal permanent residency.

WHERE DOES GRANDMA LIVE?

My grandmother was able to maintain her green card although she did not live in America. Aida and I had a wonderful relationship. I'm sure you can relate to the special bond that exists with grandparents. When I lived in Egypt, while my parents tried to reconcile their marriage, I got to know my grandmother.

Aida was a tall, elegant woman. I remember her thick, white hair that she always combed backwards. It was juxtaposed against her brilliant blue eyes. When she held my hand, I would feel the coarseness of her palm as a reminder of our modest background. They were the hands of a woman who had used them for everything from washing clothes to skinning poultry.

When she was in public, she would always wear a black dress. It symbolized her continued mourning for her husband, who passed away years before. I would always go to the market with her. Vendors lined the streets and sold everything from soap to chickens that were freshly slaughtered. Vendors would yell poetic descriptions of their products amongst the harsh smell of fresh fish out in the summer heat. The streets were crowded with women and cars. It felt like complete chaos.

Somehow, Aida maneuvered the crowded market with dignity and grace. The vendors knew her and greeted her with deference. She always got the best deals. Money was a limited commodity in my family, and she made sure it went as far as possible. She lived in a small but cozy two-bedroom apartment. It was the same apartment where she raised five children. She always proudly said that she would spend her last days in that apartment—and she was right.

The apartment always smelled of the day's lunch or a fresh-baked cake. I always considered my grandmother's house to be my home in Egypt. When I ran away from my father's house, I ran to my grandma. When I made too much noise playing outside, my grandmother was my negotiator with the neighbors. When I wanted to have my favorite meal for the millionth time, I would ask my grandma.

After we fled Egypt, I had little hope of seeing my grandmother for many years to come. We could not go back to Egypt, and my grandmother had no intention of immigrating to America. This is why I was shocked when my uncle Michael told my mother that Aida received her immigrant visa. My grandmother was coming to America.

My uncle had an immigration plan for all his siblings. It was important that my grandmother have a green card for this plan—having this, she could petition for her other children. She could do this because they were unmarried sons and daughters of a green card holder. This was faster than having my US citizen uncle petition for his brothers and sisters to come as siblings of a US citizen.

Also, if my grandmother became a US citizen, things could go even faster. She could petition for her children as unmarried sons and daughters of US citizens that are over twenty-one years of age. The Consul's Corner on family-based immigration visas can help refresh your memory on immigrant visa categories.

The problem was that Aida was not interested in living in the United States. Contrary to popular belief, not everyone who has the option of immigrating to America is jumping at the opportunity. My grandmother was one of these people. She loved her apartment in Alexandria, Egypt. Her next-door neighbor was her best friend, and she knew all the local vendors in the market. In my grandmother's mind, she had everything she needed in Alexandria. She dreaded the thought of traveling to a faraway place.

Michael explained to her how her children would benefit if she had a green card. Since it would be faster to receive immigrant visas if their mother was the petitioner rather than their brother, Aida felt like she had an obligation to do this for her family. Like most parents, Aida gave in to her son's appeals. She made the sacrifice and immigrated to America.

Aida arrived in John F. Kennedy International Airport in New York City. She told me that when she arrived at JFK, she cried from fear. Accustomed to the small town of Alexandria, she was suddenly in the middle of the Big Apple.

When my grandmother arrived in New Jersey, it was a momentous occasion for me. She lived with Michael in a studio apartment. Both my uncle and mother worked and, therefore, could not spend much time with her during the day. Since she did not speak English very well and was not very daring, she did not venture out into Jersey City alone. She spent a lot of time looking out a window with a view of John F. Kennedy Boulevard and Lincoln Park in Jersey City.

I was a freshman in high school, and my uncle lived two blocks away from my school. When possible, I would pass by my uncle's house to spend my lunch period with Aida. I had to take advantage of her presence in New Jersey because she was not always there.

Once she arrived in the US, she filed the application for her green card. US Citizenship and Immigration Services (USCIS) issues green cards in America. USCIS interviews the applicant and, if there are no issues, mails the green card to the person's US home address.

Shortly after receiving her green card in the mail, my grandmother traveled back to Egypt. Among immigrant communities, there is a name for arriving in the US to receive the green card and then leaving—it is called a "soft landing" or more simply a "landing."

It is common to hear people all over the world say "I'm going to do my landing and then come back." The reasons that immigrants do a landing vary. Some may need to go back to finish personal and business issues. Others may go back while waiting for a job to start. They are even those who just prefer to not stay in the US.

After her initial trip to the US, Aida came back about every six months. She always had the "intention" to live in the US but spent most of her time in Egypt. Although Aida had her green card, she did not actually live in America. She spent a few weeks in New Jersey and then went back to Egypt. She was visiting the US but not actually living there.

PERMANENT IS NOT REALLY PERMANENT

Aida was not alone—many people in our community had green cards but lived in Egypt. They kept their green cards valid by traveling to the US once or twice a year. This was so common that I actually thought it was normal for people to have a green card but not live in America. I later learned it was not.

Once the green card was issued, Aida had all the rights of a lawful permanent resident. It did not matter if she did not have a physical presence in the US most of the time. In theory, this should not have been possible. The constant absence demonstrated that my grandmother's intention was not really to live in America. Nonetheless, her green card remained valid. She was always allowed to enter the US as a legal permanent resident.

This meant that my grandmother enjoyed all the privileges the green card has to offer. She could travel in and out of America. She could submit a petition for her other children to come to America. She could apply for citizenship after five years if she met all other requirements. She could enjoy the benefits of lawful permanent residency without being a permanent resident.

As time passed, Aida became less and less inclined to travel to America. She got tired of the long flights between Cairo and New York. She was lonely being away from her community. One afternoon, over lunch, Aida told me that she no longer wanted to make the trips to New Jersey. She knew it meant she would not receive American citizenship.

I was surprised. American citizenship was the ultimate prize in the immigration journey, but my grandmother was willing to give it up. Soon after that conversation, my grandmother took off from JFK on Egypt Air back to Cairo. It was the last time she would make that trip.

While on vacation in Egypt, her son Michael kept trying to convince her to come back to the US and continue the immigration process. To make her feel guilty, he told her that she had the choice to help bring another family member to America. She took out a pair of scissors and cut the green card to his horror. "Now I don't have a choice," she said. That was the end of her US citizenship journey.

When it comes to legal permanent residency in the US, permanent is not really permanent. One can be outside the United States for most of the year and hold onto their green card. A green card holder that is not living in the US still maintains their benefits and privileges. It is no wonder that the "permanent" in "lawful permanent resident" is slowly disappearing.

THE GAP: LONG DISTANCE RESIDENTS

There are several gaps in our green card system, but I will focus on one, that being that there is no physical presence requirement for a green card holder to help family members immigrate to America. By physical presence, I mean physically living in the United States. There are people all over the world who hold green cards. They are not living in America, and they are not American citizens. Yet they are still able to apply for their family members to immigrate to America.

This does not make sense, nor is it in line with the intention of our lawmakers. According to the US Congress, physical presence in the United States is important. It helps green card holders become "subject to American influences." Congress believes that, with physical presence, immigrants can absorb American customs and values. Then, in turn, they can instill our values to their family members.[25]

This is nice in theory, but it is not reflected in the regulations. Green card holders don't have to be physically present to petition for family members to come to America. They only need to submit an application, provide evidence of lawful permanent residency status, and prove that the relationship with the family member is legitimate.

For example, my grandmother was not living in America. Nonetheless, she petitioned for her daughter Mary to immigrate. She submitted the application, and she had a valid green card. That took care of having evidence of lawful permanent residency. Her daughter's birth certificate could serve as evidence of a legitimate relationship. The fact that she was not actually living in the US was not a problem—she could complete the petition for her daughter without it. The requirements did not call for evidence of physical presence in America.

My grandmother was not American. She was not living in America nor did she spend significant time here. But she had the power to create a new immigrant to America. This does not reflect the intentions of our legislators. My grandmother is not alone—as part of my research for

---

25   Foreign Affairs Manual 301.7-3.

this book, I met hundreds of families. Many of them had people who have green cards but are not living in America, but one family stands out in my mind.

Remember the description of a family that I started the book with? Three generations have American citizenship or green cards but never lived in America. Let's look at their story in more detail.

Ronny immigrated to the US decades ago. He became a naturalized US citizen five years later. He petitioned for his sister Gina to immigrate to America. Gina did her landing and returned to her home country soon thereafter. She traveled to the US every six months. There were several reasons for her trip—she wanted to visit her brother in California and her younger son who was studying in New York City. She also wanted to qualify to get her US citizenship.

She used to love walking around Columbus Circle and into Central Park. She organized her trips to be in the US during the spring and the fall. She did not want to leave her husband, who was of retirement age, home alone for too long. Since he did not want to live in the US, she would make short visits and then return home to her husband.

Gina became a US citizen and petitioned for her older son,

Gilbert, to immigrate to America. Gilbert arrived in the US for his landing and then immediately returned to his home country after receiving the green card. He had a private business that he could not close. He also wanted to be present to take care of his aging parents.

Gilbert traveled to the US on a yearly basis to maintain his green card. He continued to have a valid green card although he did not live in America. Gilbert got married to Marina. He did not petition for his wife to become a green card holder; instead, she received a tourist visa. When they traveled together to the US, he would go as a green card holder, and she would go as a tourist visa holder.

A few years later, their first son was conceived. Marina traveled to the US using her tourist visa that she received before to give birth to their son, Mark. Since Mark was born in the US, he became a US citizen through birthright citizenship. Two years later, their daughter, Mia, was born in their home country.

Gilbert decided to petition for his wife and daughter to become green card holders. He was able to do so although he was not living in America. His wife and daughter received immigrant visas. Marina and Mia then traveled to the US to do their landings and received their green cards. Afterward, they traveled back to their home country, where they still live. Gilbert and his family intend to live in the US, but they are not sure when. For now, they are legal permanent residents of the US living in a foreign country.

To summarize, Gina became a naturalized US citizen without spending significant time in America. Her son Gilbert received a green card but never lived in America. Gilbert petitioned for his wife and daughter (who also did not live in the US) to become green card holders. Their son, Mark, became a US citizen thanks to birthright citizenship, but he did not live in the US

Amazingly, three generations of one family are either US citizens or legal permanent residents—yet none of them ever lived in America. They are not alone. How can our laws allow this?

CLOSING THE GAP: MAKE PERMANENT PERMANENT

I recommend proposing a new regulation to US Citizenship and Immigration Services. It adds a physical presence requirement for green card holders that want to petition for family members to immigrate to America. They would have to be physically present in the US for at least twelve consecutive months immediately before applying. Green card holders that are not living in the US would not be able to petition for other family members to immigrate to America.

For example, Carole is a green card holder from Canada. She wants to petition for Roger to immigrate to America.

YOU BE THE CONSUL

Now it's time for you to be the consul. Imagine you are a consular officer at the US embassy in Bucharest. You are interviewing a family-based immigrant visa applicant. The applicant's sponsor is their spouse, who has had a green card for the past year.

The visa application is complete. The application includes a copy of the spouse's valid green card. A copy of the marriage certificate proves that the relationship is valid. The financial sponsorship forms are also correct.

The applicant's security clearance checks out. The interview with the applicant does not reveal any issues. There is no evidence that the green card holder who applied for the spouse is physically present in America. But it does not matter because it is not required as part of the application. Do you issue the immigrant visa?

Yes, you would issue the visa. The green card of the petitioner is valid. All the documentation is correct. The applicant passed all the clearances.

You correctly follow the procedures and issue the visa. The fact that the petitioner may not actually be living in the US is not accounted for under current policies. In reality, you may have issued a green card to someone who has no true intentions of living in America.

But since she spends most of her time living in Canada, she does not qualify to petition for Roger. She will only qualify to bring Roger to America once she has lived in the US for twelve consecutive months.

This proposed regulation is useful for several reasons. It supports Congress's vision of physical presence, prevents green card holders that are not living in the US from bringing other family members to America, and rewards green card holders that are living in America. The reward is they will have the right to petition for other family members to join them.

IMPLEMENTATION

Implementing this recommendation would not be hard. It would use processes that are already in place by the US government—we would not be reinventing the wheel.

Currently, the US government already uses a physical presence requirement. It is used for green card holders who want to apply for US citizenship. To apply for US citizenship, a green card holder must show five years of continuous residency in America. This means the immigrant must have a permanent home in America. They cannot be away from this home for more than six months at a time during the five years.

The green card holder must also show that they were physically present in the US for at least half of the five years. This means that they must have been physically living in the US for thirty out of sixty months.

For example, my grandmother never spent more than six months at a time outside the US in five years. She met her continuous residency rule, but she was only physically present in the US for twenty months during the five years. She did not meet the physical presence rule and would not qualify to become a US citizen. The Consul's Corner on naturalization provides more details.

The processes that determine physical presence already exist—they are used in determining which green card holders can apply for US citizenship. These same processes can be applied to determine which green card holders can bring family members to America. Only the numbers would need to change. To apply for US citizenship, the physical presence rule is thirty out of sixty months.[26] To apply for family members to immigrate to America, the rule would become twelve out of twelve months.

A COMMON GROUND

The proposed rule is a reasonable request. The right to

---

26 For spouses of American citizens, less time is required.

apply for relatives to immigrate to America is a privilege and should not be taken for granted. If a green card holder is not living in the US, they should not have this privilege.

This is the same concept that already applies to green card holders who want to apply for US citizenship. If they do not complete the physical presence requirements, they cannot apply for citizenship.

This recommendation aligns with the intentions of our lawmakers. Congress believes that physical presence in America is important. Immigrants absorb American customs and values while living in America. A physical presence rule on green card holders to petition for family members would work towards that vision.

It would also reward green card holders who are living in America. They can exercise two important privileges that others cannot—they can help family members immigrate and can become US citizens.

CONCLUSION

Green card holders can help family members immigrate to the US, even if they are not living in America. This is not good policy—green card holders can enjoy their most important rights as lawful permanent residents without actually being residents. Since my grandmother was not living in America, she should not have been able to petition for her daughter to immigrate.

We need a physical presence rule for green card holders to bring family members to America. There should be no more examples of generations of the same family becoming US citizens and legal permanent residents without living in America. Let's move towards a more pro-American immigration policy.

In the next chapter, we will create the Pro-American Immigration Plan. To do so, we will summarize all the gaps that we discussed in the previous chapters. We will see how the recommendations made to address all these gaps come together in one plan that will strengthen our legal immigration processes.

THE CONSUL'S CORNER: LAWFUL PERMANENT RESIDENCY AND NATURALIZATION

Green card holders may lose their green cards if they

- Move to another country, intending to live there permanently.

- Remain outside of the United States for an extended period of time (over twelve months), unless the intention is a temporary absence, as shown by

  ◦ The reason for the trip;

  ◦ The amount of time intended to be absent from the United States;

  ◦ Circumstances of the absence; and

  ◦ Any events that may have prolonged the absence.

- Fail to file income tax returns while living outside of the United States for any period.

- Being a "nonimmigrant" on US tax returns.

- An immigration judge issues a final removal order.

Green card holders may apply for family members to immigrate to the US by

- Filing Form I-130, Petition for Alien Relative.

- Providing proof of their status as a permanent resident.

- Submitting evidence of the qualifying relationship such as a birth certificate, marriage certificate, divorce decree, etc.

- Submitting proof of any legal name changes

Requirements for green card holders to become US citizens include the following:

- Be at least eighteen years old at the time of application

- Be a permanent resident (have a green card) for at least five years

- Demonstrate continuous residence (no absences of more than six months) in the US for at least five years immediately preceding the application

- Demonstrate being physically present in the US for at least thirty months out of the five years immediately preceding the date of application

- Live for at least three months in the state or USCIS district of application

- Be able to read, write, and speak basic English

- Have a basic understanding of US history and government

- Be a person of good moral character

- Demonstrate an attachment to the ideals of the US Constitution.

*Data provided by the United States Citizenship and Immigration Services (USCIS)

https://www.uscis.gov/family/family-green-card-holders-permanent-residents

CHAPTER 9

---- ★ ----

PRO-AMERICAN IMMIGRATION PLAN

INTRODUCTION

The Great Seal of the United States is adorned with an eagle. It has an olive branch in its right talon, arrows in its left talon, and a ribbon in its beak. On the ribbon is inscribed the Latin phrase "E Pluribus Unum," or "Out of Many, One." The phrase is a cornerstone in America's history and society. Out of thirteen colonies, we became one country. Out of many peoples, we are one nation.

Supreme Court Justice Ruth Bader Ginsburg spoke about the importance of "E Pluribus Unum." While delivering the oath of allegiance to a group of immigrants becoming naturalized US citizens, she said, "We are a nation made strong by people like you." In other words, out of many immigrants emerges one resilient nation.

There are some assumptions in this statement. We assume that immigrants come to America in line with the nation's immigration laws. We assume that our resilient nation has an immigration policy that prioritizes the necessities of its citizens. We assume the United States is seen as a beacon of freedom and opportunity all over the world. In fact, this last assumption is the reason my family and I immigrated to America.

With these assumptions, we can create a fuller vision of "E Pluribus Unum." If the immigrants who come to the United States do so in line with the nation's immigration laws, our nation becomes stronger. With an immigration policy that prioritizes the necessities of its citizens, and recognizes the desire for people to pursue the American dream, we will truly be living up to our country's ideals.

This is how I interpret "E Pluribus Unum"—but this vision seems to not always be the case in practice. As we've seen, there are holes in our immigration policy that challenge it.

In this chapter, I summarize the current gaps in our legal immigration policy that we covered. In response to the gaps, I will lay out the Pro-American Immigration Plan. The plan strengthens US immigration policy and takes into account the interests of Americans first. It offers a win-win scenario to the various stakeholders in the immigration process. Most importantly, it offers an actionable compromise in the immigration debate.

PRO-FOREIGNER IMMIGRATION POLICIES

All Americans expect their government to draft and implement laws that are pro-American. Regardless of our political views, economic backgrounds, or physical locations, we expect that our laws focus on our interests. We expect that our security laws prioritize our security first. We expect that our trade laws protect our economy first. We expect that our financial laws improve the lives of Americans first.

The same is true about immigration laws—we expect that our immigration laws focus on the necessities of the United States and its citizens first. There may be disagreement on immigration priorities, with some Americans wanting to restrict it and others wanting to expand it. In spite of our disagreement on particular issues, all Americans want immigration policies that are pro-American.

Americans want to welcome immigrants into the United States, but we want to do it in a way that is controlled and consistent with our laws. As we have seen in the previous chapters, there are five immigration rules that do not put the needs of the United States first. They are more to the advantage of foreigners than Americans. These are parts of our immigration regulations that are not pro-American.

1. Foreigners who abuse birthright citizenship are rewarded with more visas to America. The same foreigners who use a tourist visa to give birth in the US continue to receive more tourist visas for further travel. The law is being interpreted in a way that is more beneficial to foreigners than to Americans.

    The adjudication of US tourist visa is made under law INA 214(b). It requires consular officers to presume that every visa applicant is an intending immigrant, so the applicant must demonstrate strong ties to a country other than America.

    By having a baby in the US, the parents then have a child who is an American citizen. The parents took a tangible action to establish ties with America, since a person's child tends to be their strongest tie. If tourist visa applicant's strongest tie, or most important element in their life, is a US citizen, they cannot overcome the assumption that they are intending immigrants. They should not qualify for a further tourist visa.

    In spite of this, consular officers are issuing thousands of visas to foreign mothers and fathers who have delivered babies in America. This is encouraging foreigners to continue to use birthright citizenship in a way that is not in line with the intention of the law.

2. The financial requirements to serve as a sponsor for an immigrant also qualify that same sponsor for welfare. The income requirement to sponsor an immigrant is 125 percent of the federal poverty level. The threshold to qualify for US government assistance is 130 percent of the federal poverty level. This means that some of the sponsors of immigrants also qualify for public assistance. This is not in line with immigration law, as US policy states, that immigrants who come to the US must "not depend on public resources to meet their needs."

   The law requires all sponsors and immigrants to be self-sufficient. They are not eligible for public assistance programs. But, the financial sponsorship requirement allows people to sponsor immigrants with annual income levels that would also qualify them for welfare programs.

3. It is easier for a fiancé to immigrate to America than a spouse. There is no rule that a US citizen fiancé must take financial responsibility for their foreign fiancé. It is up to the consular officer to request proof that the foreign fiancé, and any children they bring with them,

will not be a pubic charge. Yet, in contrast, sponsors of spouses must provide an affidavit of support in the immigration process.

If an affidavit of support is, indeed, requested, the sponsor for the fiancé only has to make 100 percent of the federal poverty level. This is much less than the financial requirement to sponsor a spouse (125 percent of the federal poverty level). This means that, after getting married, the new spouse may not even qualify for their green card—they may not be able to meet the additional financial sponsorship requirements. This could then lead to the individual's deportation, which is problematic for American taxpayers.

The financial sponsorship requirements for fiancés are also not consistent with the public charge law. It is less than the threshold to qualify for public assistance (130 percent of the federal poverty level). To summarize, the foreign fiancé sponsorship requirements are well below the family-based immigration sponsorship and the minimum public charge requirements—and this needs to change.

4. The diversity visa program does not take into consideration how the immigrant will benefit the American economy. Each year, the diversity visa lottery allows 50,000 immigrants to come to America. To apply,

the applicant must come from a qualifying country and have a high school diploma or two years of work experience in the past five years. If their application number is selected, the foreigner, along with their spouse and children, gets a green card to come to America.

This is an amazing opportunity for the foreigner. They win the lottery, and the reward is a green card. The United States may not be as lucky—there is no way to confirm that these winners will serve the needs of the US economy. Issuing 50,000 diversity immigrant visas each year without articulating how these lottery winners will benefit the United States is problematic.

5. Green card holders who are not living in the United States are able to bring family members to America. There is no physical presence requirement for green card holders to petition for their family members. In other words, a green card holder is able to petition for their family to come to America, even if they are not living in America.

There are tens of thousands, if not hundreds of thousands, of people all over the world who hold green cards and are not physically living in our country. Permitting green card holders to petition for family members without having a US physical presence requirement is not consistent with the intentions of Congress.

These gaps in our immigration policies are not pro-American. But this is not to say that there is a conspiracy by our legislators to have policies that are not in our interests. Many of these policies and regulations have simply become obsolete over time. Some regulations have not been updated in years, decades, or even a century. It is only natural that old policies would no longer serve the modern national interest.

While we cannot change the past, we can determine the future of immigration policy. We have uncovered some of the policies that are not in the interest of the American people—now let's change them. Let's introduce new regulations that enforce our immigration laws in a way that is pro-American.

PRO-AMERICAN IMMIGRATION PLAN

Immigrating to the United States and becoming an American citizen is a privilege. This privilege is afforded to people from all over the world thanks to the generosity and hospitality of the American people. We need strong, thoughtful laws that ensure that immigration occurs in a way that is in the interest of the American people. These laws cannot be vulnerable to manipulation or exploitation.

The new regulations recommended throughout this book are intended to strengthen US immigration policy. They take into account the interests of all Americans based on common sense. Let's now assemble all the recommendations into one inclusive plan.

Recommendation one: Refuse birthright citizenship manipulators. Birthright citizenship manipulators are mothers and fathers who give birth in the United States on tourist visas to benefit from US birthright citizenship laws. These parents want to provide their children with American citizenship. They want all the benefits for their children that come with American citizenship. While they are not acting illegally, they are not acting within the intention of the law.

I propose a new rule to deny further tourist visas to these parents under law INA 214(b). By having a child in the US, the parents took tangible action to establish a strong connection with America. Since they cannot overcome the assumption that they are intending immigrants, they will not qualify for a tourist visa. This is a strict and valid interpretation of INA 214(b). Consular officers should use the guideline of the law to decide on the visa applications of parents who exploited birthright citizenship.

The parents may still qualify for work visas, immigrant visas, and student visas, but not for tourist visas. They will never again enter the US for business, medical, or touristic reasons. This make some foreign parents think twice before delivering in America. It will show that the United States is serious in moving towards the true intention behind birthright citizenship.

Recommendation two: Increase financial sponsorship requirements for family-based immigrants. The financial requirement to sponsor an immigrant is inconsistent with immigration law. It allows people to sponsor immigrants with annual income levels that also qualify them for public assistance programs.

I propose a rule to raise the annual income requirements to sponsor an immigrant from 125 percent to at least 150 percent of the federal poverty level. This removes the automatic qualification of some immigrants to receive public assistance. The annual income rule to sponsor an immigrant would then be higher than the annual income limits to qualify for welfare.

This regulation enforces immigration law INA 212(a)(4). The law states immigrants cannot be dependent on government funding. The financial requirements to sponsor an immigrant must be in line with this law.

Recommendation three: Treat fiancés like spouses. Foreign fiancés come to the US to marry American citizens and settle in America. They are immigrants, but they do not have the same sponsorship requirements as other family-based immigrants. This creates a situation in which fiancés are coming to America without a financial sponsor. There is no guarantee that they will not be a public charge. It could also mean they may not qualify for a green card in the future and should be deported.

I propose a new rule that makes the fiancé visa applicants follow the family-based immigrant sponsorship rules. This includes requiring an immigrant visa affidavit of support (Form I-864) from a US citizen. This will provide a formalized sponsorship process and guarantee that there is a US citizen that is financially responsible for the immigrant. It will also ensure that all green card requirements are met before the fiancé comes to America.

This regulation enforces immigration law INA 212(a)(4). The law states that immigrants cannot be dependent on government funding. It uses the same sponsorship process that is used for spouses of US citizens. Since fiancés are just future spouses, they should be treated the same way as spouses of American citizens in the immigration process.

Recommendation four: Meritize the diversity visa lottery. Each year, the US government selects 50,000 diversity visa winners who may immigrate to America with their families. However, there is no consideration of the economic benefits the US will gain from the lucky immigrants.

I propose a new rule that meritizes the diversity visa lottery program based. The applicant's ability to meet the needs of the US economy will be part of their qualification to win the diversity visa.

This proposed regulation would support the enforcement of the Immigration Act of 1990. The rule aligns the diversity visa program with a clearly articulated immigration strategy. This recommendation also introduces merit into the US immigration process without changing the entire immigration system.

The Department of State can use the reports already published by the Department of Labor to determine the American labor market needs. These reports include the Employment Projections Report and the Occupational Outlook Handbook. The market needs identified in these reports can be reflected in the diversity visa lottery application process.

Recommendation five: Implement a physical presence rule for green card holders who want to bring family members to America. There are many non-US citizens who, despite not living in the US, are petitioning for their family members to immigrate.

I propose a new rule to implement a physical presence requirement. The green card holder will have to live in America for at least twelve consecutive months immediately before submitting a petition. This means that a green card holder can only begin petitioning for a relative once they prove they have met this requirement.

This regulation enforces the Immigration and Nationality Act that already exists. It draws from the physical presence requirement that already exists for green card holders that are applying for US citizenship. The process could be the same but the physical presence requirement would be different.

The following figure illustrates all the proposed rules of the Pro-American Immigration Plan:

Refuse Birthright Citizenship Manipulators
Denying tourist visas to parents who delivered babies in the US using a tourist visa in the past.

Physical Presence Requirement for LPRs to Petition for Family
LPRs can begin petitioning for a relative only once they have physically lived in the US for twelve months immediately preceding the petition application.

Pro-American Immigration Plan

Increase Financial Sponsorship Requirements
Change the minimum annual income requirements to sponsor an immigrant from 125% to at least 150% of the federal poverty level based on the household size.

Meritize the Diversity Visa Lottery
The skills needed for the US economy should be taken into account as part of the applicant's qualifications to win the diversity visa.

Treat Fiancés Like Spouses
Require fiancés to provide the immigrant visa affidavit of support (Form I-864) from a US citizen for their application to be processed.

Figure 3: Pro-American Immigration Plan

ACTIONABLE COMPROMISE

The Pro-American Immigration Plan is an actionable compromise in the immigration debate that will strengthen our legal immigration process. The plan is actionable because the American people can take action to implement it immediately. In the final chapter, we will see exactly how to take action.

Not all desired changes to immigration policy are actionable. For example, there are many people who want to end birthright citizenship. But to do so would require a Supreme Court decision and, maybe, even an amendment to the Constitution. It is hard for the American people to actually make this happen.

The Pro-American Immigration Plan is a compromise because it finds a common ground among the various stakeholders in the immigration debate. Americans who are in favor of expanding immigration win, since these recommendations provide a sensible alternative to stopping some immigration programs altogether. One only has to look to recommendation four, which meritizes the diversity visa program. The program will continue to welcome 50,000 immigrants per year and, in effect, keep America's doors open to people who would not otherwise have an opportunity to immigrate.

Americans who are in favor of restricting immigration also win—these recommendations strengthen our policies and make it more difficult to manipulate the process. The plan would prevent green card holders who are not living in America from petitioning for their family members to immigrate. With more robust laws, policymakers have more control over the immigration process. They would be able to control the flow of legal immigrants in a way that reflects America's priorities.

Institutions involved in the immigration process win as

well. For example, since the plan treats fiancés as family-based immigrants, they would have to follow the same financial sponsorship requirements as spouses. This would reduce both public charge issues and the possibility that the fiancé will not qualify for a green card and, therefore, have to be deported. Immigration courts will be able to save their time, money, and human resources.

In this plan, even immigrants win. The plan is to the advantage of immigrants who genuinely make America their home. Millions of green card holders are living, working, and paying taxes in America. Many of them want to bring family members to America, and it is not fair for them to wait in line behind other green card holders who are not living here. By adding a physical presence rule for green card holders to petition for family members, what I am proposing will fix that.

The plan strengthens our immigration process. It aligns immigration rules with immigration laws. While most Americans assume this is already the case, we have seen there are several areas in which the rules to immigrate are not in line with US immigration law.

The Pro-American Immigration Plan provides reasonable, feasible solutions that we can realistically act on. These solutions help eliminate the gaps in our immigration policy that are problematic for both Americans and the immigrants who want to make America their home. The recommendations presented carve out a common ground in the immigration policy debate. All stakeholders win through these modest, but uncompromising, steps that are pro-American.

CONCLUSION

Throughout this book, I shared my family's immigration story and my experience as a US consul. I shed light on five gaps in US immigration policy that put the United States and Americans at a disadvantage. I also presented the Pro-American Immigration Plan, which outlines five new regulations that can be proposed to our government agencies. I put this plan together to put a new perspective on the immigration debate. These regulations fill the gaps to make our immigration policy more pro-American.

The plan is an actionable compromise in the immigration discussion. It aims to accommodate the views of Americans on both sides of the debate. It puts the interests of all Americans at the forefront of the solution. It is not the final word on immigration, but it can be the start of a larger conversation.

If I did my job, then you should have a clearer idea about how foreigners legally immigrate to America and a sense of some of the shortcomings of our immigration policy.

Hopefully, you also have ideas for new rules to enforce our existing laws in a way that address these shortcomings.

I hope that I sparked your interest in helping to bring reasonable reform to our immigration policy. In the next, and final, chapter, I will ask you to take action. We will look at ways in which you can help to fill these gaps.

CHAPTER 10

——— ⭐ ———

CALL TO ACTION

Diplomats get invited to many receptions and private events with people of power. They often find themselves in the company of heads of state, parliamentarians, ministers, religious leaders, and others whose decisions affect nations.

I attended a dinner in the home of a longtime parliamentarian. A parliamentarian is similar to a congressperson in the American political system. It was an intimate dinner with only twelve people. Among them were his wife, some of his advisors, and close friends. Although it was a small dinner, it was a lavish event.

The home was on top of a hill with an exquisite garden that overlooked the Mediterranean Sea. The dinner table was immense, with each place setting perfectly arranged. The table centerpiece had freshly cut gardenia flowers floating in a crystal bowl with a touch of rose water. The infusion of the flowers with the rose water created a delightful natural air freshener.

A team of butlers methodically brought out each course. They worked in perfect synchronicity so that the service was like a choreographed dance. Each course was accompanied by a local wine chosen to make flavors stand out in the palate. This was a far cry from the small dinner table we picked up from a garbage can that I ate on in Jersey City.

During the extravagant event, we discussed local and American politics and culture. One of the advisors to the parliamentarian forcefully expressed his opinion. He declared that, after September 11, America was no longer the land of opportunity. He asserted that this was especially true for people of Middle Eastern backgrounds. I found it ironic that, out of all people, he was telling this to me.

I disagreed with him and explained that I was an immigrant to America from Egypt. A single mother on welfare raised me because my father abandoned us. I ate government cheese and went to public schools. The only reason I could be invited to the home of a foreign dignitary and attend such a lavish dinner as a US diplomat is that America continues to be the land of opportunity.

There is no doubt that I benefited from immigrating to America. I am reminded of this every day. I wish the same for people from all over the world who want to legally pursue the American dream.

I also have a strong desire to see US immigration policy that puts the needs of Americans first. This want is inspired by the oath of office I took to bear true faith and allegiance to the Constitution and the American people.

US immigration policy should not have gaps that allow three generations of the same family to be American citizens or US green card holders without having ever lived in the United States. Our legal immigration process must protect American interests, keep our country safe, and allow for immigrants to come to America in a controlled way that is consistent with the law.

In this chapter, I will provide you with a plan of action if you want to participate in strengthening our immigration policy. Let's show our legislators that we all want a more pro-American immigration policy.

A REASONABLE COMMON GROUND

It is important that the people on both sides of the immigration debate look at the issue from the opposing side as well. Americans who want to open the immigration door wider should realize that the United States is not able to take in everyone who wants to come to our country.

Millions of people are hoping to come to America. They want to escape conflict and persecution or make a better life for themselves. In 2018, a record high of 70.8 million people around the world were forcibly displaced.[27] Every day, 37,000 people are forced to flee their homes because of conflict and persecution. In Venezuela, 2.6 million people alone have poured out of the country since 2015.[28] Given the opportunity, almost all these people would come to America, but there is not enough capacity to accept them.

At the same time, Americans who want to stop immigration should realize that this would be a disservice to the United States. Immigration is the secret sauce that makes America special. For decades, the United States has distinguished itself from other major economies in the world—and not only because of our military might or economic prowess.

America offers something that no other country does—a dream. The United States harnesses international talent because it captures people's imaginations and aspirations. This helps us stay ahead of other major economies like

27   Grandi, "Forced displacement in 2018."

28   Bahar, "Latin America is facing a refugee crisis."

China, India, and Japan. Immigration has helped some of the best minds come and contribute to America.

Understanding the opposite side on the immigration debate does not mean you must adopt the other perspective. But I do hope that it creates an understanding that the extreme end of both sides is not attainable. We cannot let all immigrants into the United States, just as we cannot slam the door shut on all immigrants.

We need a more reasonable common ground in the immigration debate. The common ground should make sense for all Americans and immigrants who are acting in the spirit of the law. This begins with ensuring the United States has a pro-American immigration policy that puts the interests of all Americans first.

TAKING ACTION

If you share in the Pro-American Immigration Plan that I outlined, I ask you to take action. If you disagree with some of the recommendations, I hope you will take action on the areas where you do agree. You can take action by joining me in petitioning our government agencies. Our petition will be to create new rules to enforce the immigration laws that are already in place.

Our right to petition the government is protected under

the Constitution. The First Amendment of the Constitution protects the right of the American people "to petition the Government for a redress of grievances." The right to petition is right up there with freedom of religion, speech, press, and assembly.

Our government agencies must allow constituents to submit petitions for new rules. The Administrative Procedure Act (APA) ensures this can happen. It requires government agencies to have a process for people to petition for the issuance, amendment, or repeal of a rule. The APA also requires that agencies decide on petitions within a reasonable amount of time.

The petition process begins with submitting a "Petition for Rulemaking." The petition includes the new rule and justification. Private individuals, groups of citizens, or lobbying organizations can submit petitions. The petition is then sent to the appropriate government agency depending on the type of regulation being proposed. For example, a regulation on tourist visa processing would go to the Department of State. A regulation on pollution would go to the Environmental Protection Agency (EPA). A regulation on job creation would go to the Department of Commerce.

Next, the agency decides if the proposed regulation makes sense. If so, it issues a notice of proposed rulemaking. The proposed regulation is listed in the US Federal Register so members of the public can comment. The time for comment varies, but usually it is between sixty and 180 days. People from around the country may give their comments to support it or to recommend changes.

After public commentary, the agency will take the comments into consideration. It makes revisions to the proposed regulation as needed. Once the text is finalized, the agency issues the final regulation. It is published in the Federal Register and on the website https://www.regulations.gov. The new regulation is then sent to Congress before it takes effect.

Congress usually has sixty days to review the regulation. Congress can void the new rule. To do so, it must pass a resolution of disapproval and have the president sign it. However, it is extremely rare for Congress to disapprove of a new regulation. During the period from 1996–2016, there were 84,186 regulations enacted by different government agencies, and Congress disapproved of only one.

Once the regulation passes the Congressional review period, it becomes part of the code of federal regulations. The following figure is a summary of the steps and amount of time needed for a new regulation to go from a proposal to an enforceable rule:

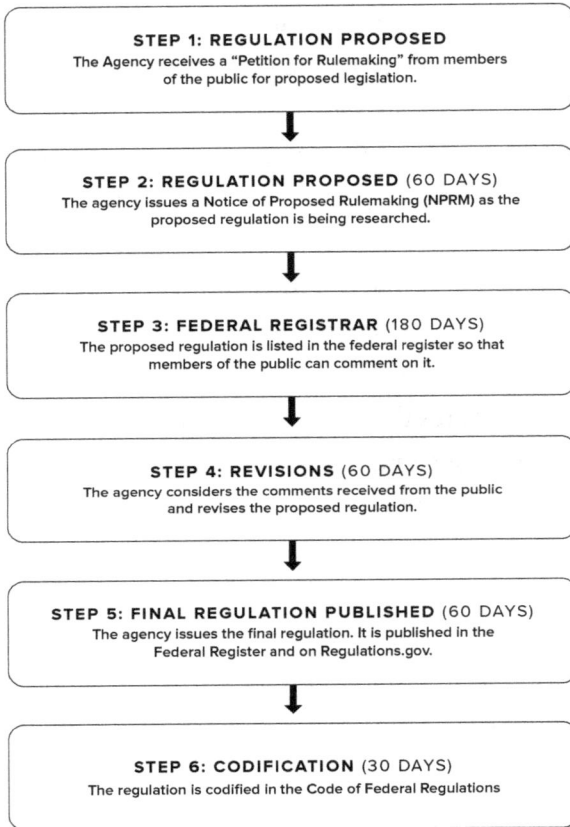

STEP 1: REGULATION PROPOSED
The Agency receives a "Petition for Rulemaking" from members of the public for proposed legislation.

STEP 2: REGULATION PROPOSED (60 DAYS)
The agency issues a Notice of Proposed Rulemaking (NPRM) as the proposed regulation is being researched.

STEP 3: FEDERAL REGISTRAR (180 DAYS)
The proposed regulation is listed in the federal register so that members of the public can comment on it.

STEP 4: REVISIONS (60 DAYS)
The agency considers the comments received from the public and revises the proposed regulation.

STEP 5: FINAL REGULATION PUBLISHED (60 DAYS)
The agency issues the final regulation. It is published in the Federal Register and on Regulations.gov.

STEP 6: CODIFICATION (30 DAYS)
The regulation is codified in the Code of Federal Regulations

Figure 4: Process to Establish a Regulation

The critical step in this process is successfully lobbying a government agency to adopt a regulation. Once this is done, there is a very good chance that it will be adopted and become the standard used to enforce existing immigration laws. It is possible that, in approximately one year from the time a proposed regulation is put on an agency's agenda, it will begin to take effect.

A UNIFIED, AMPLIFIED, AND COHERENT VOICE

We may have the legal authority to petition our government and express our opinions, but it does not mean the process is easy. The APA does not specify the procedures agencies must follow to consider petitions. To get the attention of government agencies, we must be able to speak in a unified, amplified, and coherent voice.

This approach is important because there is strength in numbers. Each person may contact their representative or petition a government agency on their own. However, the reality is that an individual letter or petition will probably not get too much attention. On the White House website, it states that an official response will be provided for petitions with at least 100,000 signatures gathered in thirty days. As can be imagined, the White House sets the example for other government agencies.

But the dynamics change when individuals who share the same feelings come together. Broad support from a large and diverse group of people strengthens the petition. It demands the attention of the agency the petition is being addressed to and increases the chance it is added to the agency's regulations review committee.

Our voice must also be amplified since there is a lot of clamor in the immigration debate. The vast majority of it focuses on illegal immigration. Certain politicians want to make it legal for immigrants to enter the US without documentation. Others want to remove the threat of deportation of millions of undocumented people in America. Many more want to do everything possible to not allow immigrants to enter the US illegally. The debate on illegal immigration is important, but it is not addressing the gaps that we already have in our legal immigration system. We need to make our voice heard about the shortcomings in our legal immigration system.

Our message must be coherent. I know people who think the United States should take responsibility for all migrants and refugees in the world. At the same time, I know people who would love to put a "no vacancies" sign on the Statue of Liberty. But these extreme views are not consistent with the world in which we are currently living. More than anything, we should want the requirements to immigrate to the US to be consistent with our legal immigration laws and framework. We should want to eliminate the gaps in immigration policy that are being manipulated. This is a reasonable and coherent message for all.

JOIN THE PRO-AMERICAN IMMIGRATION MOVEMENT

At the beginning of the book, I laid out our goal. We want to propose new immigration rules that are pro-American. The proposed rules will be directed to the Department of

State and US Citizenship & Immigration Services. They will enforce our current laws, but in a way that is more beneficial to Americans.

To do this, we need to get our recommendations on the agenda of these agencies. To get the attention of our government, we need to speak in a unified voice. To help make this happen, I created a website: www.proamericanimmigration.com.

On the website, you can select the recommendations presented in this book that you agree with. Then you can electronically sign a petition for the particular recommendations that you selected. Our goal is to have a pro-American immigration team that consists of at least 500,000 people. Once we reach our goal, we will submit official petitions for rulemaking to the appropriate government agency. You will be part of the process each step of the way.

Petitioning our government will not be easy. As we saw, the process for a new rule to go from conception to code includes several steps and could take a year or more. However, that does not mean it is not worth trying. Over one million people use the legal immigration system to come to America every year. These are the majority of immigrants that enter our country, and this process deserves our attention.

There are gaps in legal immigration regulations. They can be manipulated to the disadvantage of Americans and must be fixed. Change is needed to make sure the rules to immigrate to America are consistent with our law. But change does not start with politicians; it starts with people like you. Help us be the voice for pro-American immigration.

Part of Our Immigration Tree

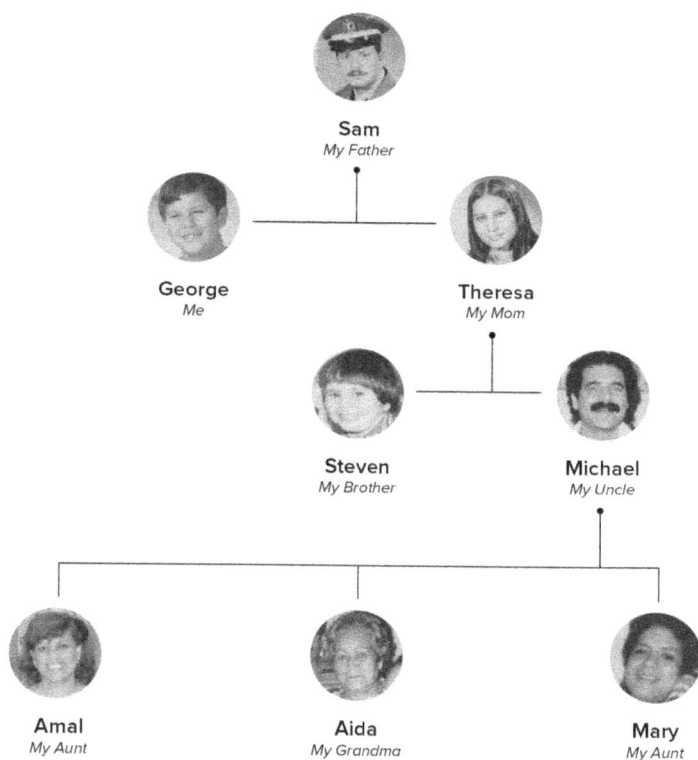

Sam
My Father

George
Me

Theresa
My Mom

Steven
My Brother

Michael
My Uncle

Amal
My Aunt

Aida
My Grandma

Mary
My Aunt

ACKNOWLEDGMENTS

My life could have turned out so much differently. I am blessed that it didn't. I want to thank some great people who guided me along the way:

My family in the United States and Egypt for the love.

My brother, Steven, for staying close in spite of the distance.

My surrogate father, Samer, for always believing in the American dream.

The folks who gave us government cheese and butter for being unsung heroes.

Dr. Soffie Zaki for keeping us healthy even when we couldn't afford it.

Dr. Robert Perry and the Pre-Cap team for keeping us off the street and making education our focus.

Ms. Sharon Felton and everyone at Academic High School for the structure amidst the chaos.

Dr. Robert Rubinstein for keeping me in when everyone wanted me out.

Tucker Max and the Scribe team for helping make a dream of writing a book a reality.

My best friends, you know who you are, for constantly believing in me.

Omar Jheir and the Sip Team for always saving me a place for me to write.

My brothers and sisters at the Department of State and Department of Defense for serving our country with honor.

God for always keeping hope on the horizon.

Thank you all!

BIBLIOGRAPHY

Anderson, Stuart. "Immigrants and Billion Dollar Startups."
National Foundation for American Policy (March 2016): 1.

Bahar, Dany. "Latin American Is Facing a Refugee Crisis." Foreign
Affairs (October 2018). https://www.foreignaffairs.com/articles/
venezuela/2018-10-23/latin-america-facing-refugee-crisis.

Bush, George W. "President Bush Addresses the Nation on
Immigration Reform." White House Archives. May 2006.
https://georgewbush-whitehouse.archives.gov/news/
releases/2006/05/text/20060515-8.html.

Camarota, Steven. "Trump's right. End the diversity visa lottery."
Los Angeles Times. November 2, 2017. https://www.latimes.com/
opinion/op-ed/la-oe-camarota-diversity-visa-lottery-20171102-
story.html.

Cotton, Tom, and David Purdue. "Reforming American
Immigration for a Strong Economy Act (RAISE Act):
A Bill to Raise Working Wages and Boost American
Competitiveness." August 2017. https://www.cotton.senate.
gov/?p=press_release&id=765.

Flores, René, and Ariela Schachter. "Who are the "Illegals? The Social Construction of Illegality in the United States." *American Sociological Review* (October 2018). https:doi: 10.1177/0003122418794635.

Grandi, Filippo. "Forced Displacement in 2018," UNHCR Global Trends 2018. https://www.unhcr.org/statistics/ unhcrstats/5d08d7ee7/unhcr-global-trends-2018.html.

Long, Heather. "America has a massive truck driver shortage. Here's why few want an $80,000 job." *Washington Post*. May 28, 2018. https://www.washingtonpost.com/news/wonk/ wp/2018/05/28/america-has-a-massive-truck-driver-shortage-heres-why-few-want-an-80000-job/?utm_term=.d1a6fd2080d9.

Melville, John, Janine Kaisr, and Elizabeth Brown. "Silicon Valley Competitiveness and Innovation Project." Silicon Valley Leadership Group. February 2017. https://www.svcip.com/files/ SVCIP_2017.pdf.

Min Kim, Seung. "'Fiancé visas' off limits in rush to tighten borders." Politico. December 9, 2015. https://www.politico.com/story/2015/12/ congress-fiance-visa-republicans-marriage-216570.

Muttarak, Raya, and Anthony Heath. "Who Intermarries in Britain? Explaining Ethnic Diversity in Intermarriage Patterns." *The British Journal of Sociology*. No. 61 (Spring 2010): 275–305.

Obama, Barack. "Remarks by the President on Immigration." White House Archives. June 2012. https:// obamawhitehouse.archives.gov/the-press-office/2012/06/15/ remarks-president-immigration.

Reagan, Ronald. "Statement on Signing the Immigration Reform and Control Act of 1986." Presidential Library. November 1986. https://www.reaganlibrary.gov/research/speeches/110686b.

Rubio, Marco. "Rubio & Colleagues Introduce The Border
Security, Economic Opportunity & Immigration
Modernization Act Of 2013." US Senator for Florida. April
2013. https://www.rubio.senate.gov/public/index.cfm/
press-releases?ID=85a7f16e-7b91-4f44-8c68-129ebd25a865.

Safi, Mirna, and Rogers, Godfrey. "Intermarriage and Assimilation:
Disparities in Levels of Exogamy among Immigrants in France."
Population-E. No 63 (2008): 239–268.

Schultz, Marisa. "Flood of immigrants heading for US, Central
American officials say." *New York Post*. November 25, 2016.
https://nypost.com/2016/11/25/flood-of-immigrants-heading-
for-us-central-american-officials-say/.

Scott, Rick. *Meet the Press*. February 3, 2019. https://www.nbcnews.
com/meet-the-press/meet-press-february-3-2019-n966336.

Voss, Chris, and Tahl Raz. *Never Split the Difference: Negotiating As if
Your Life Depended On It*. New York Harper Business, an imprint
of HarperCollins Publishers, 2016.

Wilkie, Christina. "Trump says he'll sign DACA deal, pursue
comprehensive immigration reform." CNBC. January 2018.
https://www.cnbc.com/2018/01/09/trump-says-hell-sign-daca-
pursue-comprehensive-immigration-reform.html.

Zong, Jie, Jeanne Batalova, and Micayla Burrows. "Frequently
Requested Statistics on Immigrants in the United States,"
Migration Policy Institute. March 2019. https://www.
migrationpolicy.org/article/frequently-requested-statistics-
immigrants-and-immigration-united-states?gclid=EAIaIQobCh
MIm6KZz7Ph3wIVxZTVCh3D8ARNEAAYASAAEgJQYfD_BwE.

ABOUT THE AUTHOR

DR. GEORGE FARAG is a former United States diplomat and consular attaché (consul). He was appointed to the diplomatic service by President George W. Bush and served at embassies throughout the Middle East.

As a consul, George interviewed thousands of people seeking immigrant and nonimmigrant visas to come to America. He decided on visa applications under US immigration law.

George was on the Consular Affairs Crisis Response team that evacuated 15,000 Americans from Beirut during the 2006 Lebanon War. He was also among the first US diplomats to enter Iraq during Operation Iraqi Freedom.

George is the recipient of the Department of State's Superior Honor Award, the Meritorious Honor Award, the George P. Schultz Consular Certificate, and the Jersey City Rotary Award. His work with the Department of State was recognized by Secretary of State Colin Powell and former Speaker of the House of Representatives Paul Ryan.

George immigrated to America from Egypt with his family. He likes to tell the story of his eighth-grade class whistling "Walk Like an Egyptian" on his first day of school. Raised by a single mother on welfare, his family struggled to survive. Since then, many good people inspired George to reach further. He is grateful to the American people for helping him pursue his American dream.

If you would like to get in touch with George, please visit his website at http://www.georgefarag.com.

www.ingramcontent.com/pod-product-compliance
Lightning Source LLC
Chambersburg PA
CBHW030241030426
42336CB00009B/200